Fishing
for
Bass

Books by A. D. Livingston

The Sky's the Limit
Poker Strategy and Winning Play
Dealing with Cheats
Fishing for Bass

Fishing for Bass:

Modern Tactics and Tackle

by A. D. Livingston

J. B. Lippincott Company
Philadelphia & New York

Chapters 20, 21, and 22 of this book have appeared in *Sports Afield*.

The quotation from "The Best Bass Fishing Starts Where Light Stops" by John Weiss is reprinted from *Sports Afield* magazine—May 1973 issue. Copyright 1973 by The Hearst Corporation. The quotation from *McClane's Standard Fishing Encyclopedia and International Angling Guide,* edited by A. J. McClane, is copyright © by Holt, Rinehart and Winston, Inc. Reprinted by permission of Holt, Rinehart and Winston, Inc.

The quotations from "Bass Boat Buyers: Beware of Brand X" by Grits Gresham and from "Oxygen Structure Fishing" are reprinted by permission from *BASSmaster* magazine, Bass Anglers Sportsman Society (B.A.S.S.), P.O. Box 3044, Montgomery, Ala. 36109.

Chapter 19 is based on Mr. Livingston's article "Catching and Keeping Large Shiners," which appeared in *Field & Stream*.

Figures 1, 2, 7, 12, and 75 through 84 courtesy of Du Pont Company. Figure 13 by Joel Arrington and Figure 29 courtesy of the North Carolina Travel and Promotion Division. Figure 18 courtesy of the Las Vegas News Bureau. Figure 21 courtesy of Ranger Boats. Figure 22 courtesy of the Garcia Corporation. Figures 24 through 27 courtesy of Jetco Incorporated. Figure 30 courtesy of Lowrance Electronics. Figure 42 courtesy of Gapen Tackle Company. Figure 47 courtesy of Best Tackle Manufacturing Company. Figure 93 courtesy of The Arnold Tackle Corporation. Figures 101 through 103 courtesy Dr. Martin Venneman. Figures 105 and 106 courtesy of *Florida Wildlife* magazine.

Photograph on page 39 courtesy of Bass Anglers Sportsman Society. Photograph on page 51 courtesy of the Ouachita Marine and Industrial Corporation. Photograph on page 86 courtesy of the South Dakota Department of Game, Fish, and Parks. Photograph on page 141 courtesy of the Texas Tourist Development Agency. Photograph on page 199 courtesy of the Tennessee Valley Authority. Photograph on page 216 by Phillip Seifert, courtesy of the Louisiana Tourist Development Commission.

All photographs not otherwise attributed are by the author.

U.S. Library of Congress Cataloging in Publication Data

Livingston, A   D   birth date
Fishing for bass: modern tactics and tackle.

1. Black bass fishing. I. Title.
SH681.L54   799.1'7'58   74–8026
ISBN–0–397–01017–6

for Howard and David

Preface

MY EDITOR SEEMED RATHER SURPRISED when I came up with a book about bass fishing. My other books had been about poker and gambling, and he wasn't expecting such a drastic change of topic. Yet, the two pursuits have much in common. As the late Jason Lucus once put it: "Fishing and poker are analogous: one has to become quite good at either to realize that, comparing one man's 'take' with another's, the element of luck is almost nonexistent; the expert nearly always gets more. There are times when even the best bass angler cannot discover many bass that are feeding, and times when even the slickest professional gambler cannot find his suckers. But there is hardly a day when the real adept at either cannot at least do well enough for eating purposes."

Lucus was right on the money, but note carefully that he qualified his statements with the terms "almost," "nearly always," and "hardly a day." There are times when the poker sharp or the bassman will have to tighten up his belt a bit. Over the long run, however, the expert will do a good deal better than the inexpert. The character traits of the expert poker player and the outstanding bass fisherman are similar. They will have patience. They will have confidence. They will be resourceful. They always concentrate on what they are doing, and on what their opponent is likely to do or not do. Finally, the poker sharp plays harder and the bassman fishes harder.

7

In this book I discuss, sometimes in fussy detail, the latest gear and tackle available to the bass angler. I have set forth many pages about lures and how to use them. I have discussed when to fish and where. And how. Ultimately, however, the bass angler will be on his own, and his success will depend not so much on the latest equipment and the hottest new lures but on how hard he fishes, on how much confidence he has, and on how well he plays the odds. But the poker analogy has an end, and the reader will be disappointed if he is looking in this book for some magic formula on how to bluff a bass into the boat!

Contents

Part One

What Every Bassman Needs (or Wants)

1

Hook and Line

THE COMPLETE BASS ANGLER of today streaks up and down the hottest new impoundment in a red-carpeted boat with a motor large enough to propel a small yacht. It is rigged with pedestal easy seats, a foot-controlled fishing motor, and enough electronic devices to intrigue even James Bond. The bassman's several free-spooling, ball-bearing, star-drag reels permit him to cast light lures and play large fish without backlashing and knuckle-busting. All his many-colored plastic worms and plugs and spoons and spinner baits and pork rinds fill a footlocker. It's not unusual these days for a bass angler to invest $5,000 in fishing equipment of one sort or another. With all this gear, the ordinary angler is apt to forget that only two things are essential to catching fish, and while attending to all his accessories he is likely to ignore his hook and abuse his line.

Most bass fishermen use monofilament line, and I have no doubt that monofilament will sometimes catch more fish than braided line will. But it will also lose more if it is not handled properly. Monofilament is tricky stuff, and the fisherman who uses it had better be very, very careful lest a big bass break loose from time to time. A knot or loop in the line, a nick from one cause or another, or a microscopic abrasion caused by rough rod

13

guides will weaken monofilament considerably—sometimes drastically. At times monofilament will break for no apparent reason, leaving the angler wondering what happened.

Just the other day, for example, I was fishing near some lily pads about 100 yards behind my house on an island in Florida's Lake Weir. I had previously taken a dozen lunkers from around the pads, and on that day I had put on a large golden shiner, hoping to interest the grandpa of the bunch. After a while the shiner started cutting up. It jumped completely out of the water. Then the float popped under, and the line zipped off fast. When I reared back to set the hook, the line popped. But it didn't break at the hook, where about 95 percent of all breaks occur. It broke about a foot or so from the end of my rod tip. I don't know why the line failed, but inspection led me to believe that I may have touched it, or come too close to it, with the end of my cigarette. Anyhow, I had connected with something solid on the other end.

Before I had rigged up again, I saw my float surface about 60 feet from the boat. I decided to up anchor and retrieve it. As I putted toward the float with my electric motor, under it went. I still had the fish hooked! I doubted that I could get it, but of course I watched all around for the float to surface again. Before too long it came up about 50 feet to the left of the boat. Using my foot control, I started the motor and eased toward it. Down it went.

I must have played hide-and-seek for fifteen minutes before I got close enough to grab the line. I won't attempt to describe my hand-over-hand battle with the fish, but it turned out to be an 8- or 9-pound largemouth! It wasn't the grandpa that I had rigged up for, but it was a pretty big one that didn't get away.

Most fishermen aren't so lucky, and I have in fact caught several lunker bass that had hooks and plastic worms inside them. The black bass isn't as acrobatic as the tarpon, and it is better compared to a line-bucking fullback (who will take to the air if he has to) than to a scatback broken field runner. Its initial surge of brute strength, together with its preference for hanging out in or near logs and limbs and other cover, makes the bass hard to stop. Many of the big ones do get away—and some that aren't so big get away too.

While an awful lot of bass are lost because the line breaks, a good many more are lost because the knot slips. Before discussing these problems in more detail, however, I would like to emphasize that not all monofilament is alike. One brand may be much better than another in one respect but much worse in another respect. It is difficult to improve one characteristic of a line without altering another, and the best the manufacturers can do is come up with a line of balanced properties. Anyhow, here are some of the things to consider when choosing a line:

Strength-to-diameter ratio. The strength of a line is expressed in the number of pounds required to break it; a 20-pound-test line will support at least 20 pounds of weight without breaking. But the pound test published on a line's label isn't the whole story. Most line makers rate their lines a bit lower than the actual laboratory tests indicate. Another point to remember is that a line is stronger when dry than when wet. A line will slowly absorb a good deal of moisture from the air or from the water, and a fully saturated line loses about 10 to 15 percent of its strength.

Other characteristics being equal, a 20-pound line with a diameter of 0.019 inch is obviously better than one with a diameter of 0.023 inch. The line with the smaller diameter will usually cast better, will be less visible to the fish, and will permit some lures with built-in action to do their thing better. But the strength-to-diameter ratio certainly isn't the only criterion for selecting a monofilament fishing line.

Stretch. The more a line stretches when one jerks on the rod, the less energy or pull available to set the hook. In other words, a line can act rather like a shock absorber. A degree of stretch is highly desirable to cushion the sudden jolt of a large fish, but most monofilament lines have too much stretch instead of not enough. Anyone who doesn't take monofilament stretch seriously should tie the end of a cheap line to a tree, back off about 40 yards, and pull on it just to see how elastic it is.

Softness. Some monofilament lines are more limp or more flexible than others. Generally, softness is a highly desirable quality in a line. A soft line is easier to cast and results in better action on some types of lure. A wiry line inhibits lure action and tends to coil excessively after it has been put on a spool, causing bird's nests during the cast. On the other hand, a line can be too soft for use on spinning and spincast reels; if a line is too limp, it will not spring off the spool correctly and may ball up under closed-face reels. A limp line also tends to slap the rod, which reduces an angler's casting distance because of friction. Generally, a very soft monofilament will also have too much stretch.

One obvious way to reduce or increase softness is to put on a lighter or a heavier line. A 10-pound line will be more limp than a 20-pound line. But there is also quite a lot of difference in softness between various brands of monofilament of the same test strength.

Knot strength. When tying monofilament line to a hook or plug eyelet, or to another line, it is most important that you use the proper knot and tie it correctly. (Various knots and how to tie them will be discussed a little later in this chapter.) But some monofilament lines do have better knot properties than others. A very soft, highly elastic line, for example, compresses under pressure and tends to slip or fail. It is also difficult to draw a knot down properly with limp monofilament.

Visibility. Monofilament line is probably not entirely invisible to bass, but it is less visible than braided line. Some monofilament line is clear, while others are tinted with one color or another. I've never been able to determine whether or not bass can tell any difference between clear or tinted line, and, frankly, I place more importance on diameter. Even so, I don't believe that visibility is as important in bass fishing as in trout fishing. Yet, I wouldn't want to go bass fishing with a plowline, and visibility is certainly a consideration when choosing a fishing line, especially when fishing plastic worms and other slow-moving lures.

For some kinds of fishing, I like to use a line that *I* can see (and which, hopefully, the bass can't see). I often use a line as a visual indicator because any twitch or change in line movement can mean that a bass has taken the lure. (Instead of striking a lure as is commonly believed, the bass usually engulfs it by opening its gills and sucking water and bait into its huge mouth, so that many strikes on still or free-falling baits are very gentle.) I can see a line twitch better when I use good polarized sunglasses, but some lines are more visible to me than others. Du Pont's fluorescent Stren line is generally considered to be more visible to the angler than most other brands are. I'm not absolutely sure how visible or invisible it is to bass, and I don't own any stock in Du Pont, but here's an argument from one of the company's technical bulletins:

> It is very easy to make the line visible to the fisherman—any bright color (red, orange, yellow, even white) is quite easy to see. Trying to make the same line invisible to the fish, however, is an entirely different matter. A brightly colored line shows up in its true color under water and even a clear monofilament will look like a black line to a fish when he sees it against the brilliant water surface in daylight.
>
> But Du Pont scientists found the answer. Instead of dyeing the nylon monofilament used in Stren, they added a fluorescent chemical which actually gives off light. It is like the fluorescent light bulbs in your home. When you turn on the electric switch the bulb glows. The "switch" for Stren fluorescent monofilament is the invisible ultraviolet rays in daylight. These rays cause Stren to glow a light blue color. At night when there is no ultraviolet light, the "switch" is turned off and Stren looks like a clear monofilament. In daylight Stren fluorescent line is a brilliant light blue color, easily visible to the fisherman against the dark water surface or shore line. Stren also glows under water but the amount of glow depends on the depth because the ultraviolet rays of the sun are filtered out by the water. Just under the surface, Stren

glows a light blue color and blends in perfectly with the reflections of the sky. It can become completely invisible to the fish rising to a surface lure from below. Ordinary monofilament looks like a dark line under these conditions.

If the fisherman is fishing deep—trolling or bottom fishing—the ultra-violet light is filtered out. The "switch" is turned off and clear Stren remains invisible against the dark background.

The author with a big largemouth that didn't get away, thanks to a sharp hook and a strong line.

No doubt other line manufacturers have other arguments. One company, for example, has said that its line is less visible to fish because it does not reflect light rays. I don't think anybody knows exactly how a bass sees a line, and, as an angling editor put it, "Theories on this factor will be kicked around until someone trains a fish to talk!"

In addition to being very careful about selecting a monofilament fishing line and being very fussy about tying it to a hook or lure, the angler also had better be cautious when fishing with the stuff. Any number of accidents —such as pinching it in the hinge of a tackle box—can cause a line to break at far below its rated pound test. To list every conceivable way of line failure would be impossible, but here are some of the more common causes, along with some conditions that alter a line's casting properties:

Abrasion. Figure 1 shows a frayed 10-pound monofilament line magnified sixty times. Believe it or not, this line would look smooth to the naked eye,

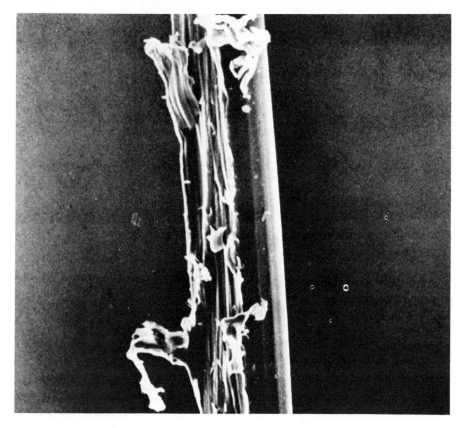

Figure 1

although it would feel rough if run between one's fingers. Normal fishing will cause abrasion to one degree or another. Pulling the line through rod tips and guides, over brush in the water, or bumping it along the bottom all cause abrasion. During the casting process, the last few inches of line really catch hell, what with the lure being stopped and snapped forward at the end of the back cast. Catching a bass will often abrade the last few inches of line drastically. It always pays to cut off a few inches of line after catching a fish or when changing lures.

Although some degree of abrasion cannot be avoided if one fishes, it can be held to a minimum by careful inspection of the line and tackle. Grooves worn in rod tips and guides may cause a line to fray and can easily weaken it by 40 or 50 percent. On spinning reels, a worn pickup bail roller or line guide can cause severe abrasion. Although the bearing surface can be smoothed down, shoeshine fashion, with tiny strips of emory paper and polished with jeweler's compounds, it is best to install a new one. Replacing them isn't a major repair job on most spinning reels, and most reputable reel manufacturers will provide spare parts at small costs.

At best, abrasion is microscopic; at worst, it falls into the category of nicks and gouges. Nicks cause stress concentration, which means that the line's strength is drastically reduced. Incidentally, it is easier to nick or abrade stiff monofilament than soft. The reason is that soft monofilament is more flexible and elastic.

Rusty eyelets. A rusty or otherwise rough hook eye or lure eyelet can cause a line to fail at far below its test strength. I asked Paul Johnson, director of research for Berkley and Company, about this problem, and here's part of their learned opinion:

> Our laboratory tests would indicate that drawing a nylon monofilament across a roughened guide surface (possibly including one that is rusty) does have a detrimental effect on the monofilament that can reduce its strength by as much as 50 percent, depending on the severity induced. Offhand, I would think these tests using line guides (not hook or lure eyelets) would be analagous to the problem you pose. Your problem, however, is further compounded by the fact that a knot is introduced into the system. During the process of tying this knot to the unsmooth or rusty eyelet, one does generate a certain amount of abrasion on the monofilament surface as it is drawn across the metal surface and then introduced into the knot region during drawing down of the knot itself. Thus, you may be talking not only of the immediate small region in contact with the rough eyelet, but also short distances of line abraded and drawn up into the knot and slightly beyond it. Under these circumstances, even the most perfectly tied fisherman's knot could yield apparently low, mystifying values.

Impact. One cause of line failure occurs when an angler sets the hook very hard into a large bass. Although impact failure sometimes occurs close to the boat, a more common cause is slack line, so that the full force of the angler's jerk hits suddenly. Plastic-worm fishermen using low-stretch line and stiff "worm rods" should be especially conscious of impact and should not set the hook until all the slack is out of the line.

Note carefully that a line's impact strength is lower than its tensile strength. Generally, the lines with high stretch are less likely to break from impact. And the more line that is out, the less the danger of impact failure.

Accidental knots. Every angler will occasionally get an overhand knot into his fishing line or leader. When he does, he had better get it out or cut the line above the knot. As indicated in Figure 2, an overhand knot causes a severe stress concentration on the outer edge of the line. Such a knot reduces a line's strength by as much as 50 percent.

Sunlight. Prolonged exposure to sunlight (or fluorescent light) makes a monofilament line brittle and difficult to cast. It also weakens it. Even though some exposure is necessary in normal fishing, an angler should avoid leaving the rod and reel in the boat or on the patio or under the rear window of a car for long periods.

Heat. Temperatures below 120 degrees F. have no permanent effect on monofilament line. Warm line, however, tends to be more flexible than cold line, so that temperature can have a bearing on a line's casting properties. Temperatures above 120 degrees F. will have a detrimental effect on

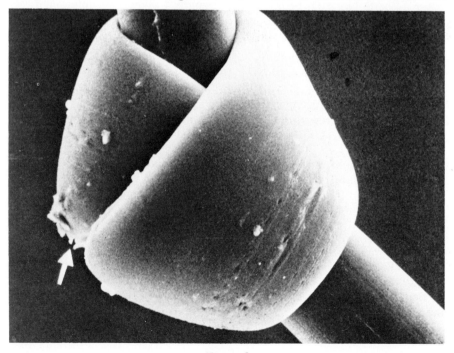

Figure 2

monofilament, but this is usually not severe until 200 degrees is reached. Nylon monofilament melts at about 500 degrees F.

Water. Neither freshwater not salt water has any *permanent* effect on the *nylon* in monofilament line. (But, as stated earlier, a line's wet strength is lower than its dry strength.) Most lines have additives to make them soft, and water will in time leach them out. Loss of the additives does not weaken the line, but it does make the line wiry and difficult to cast.

Line twist. An improperly balanced or tangled lure can cause severe line twist, especially when trolling. Another very common cause of twist among novice anglers is cranking a reel handle without taking in line, as when a large fish is making the drag slip. Twist can occur quite fast; reels having a 5-to-1 retrieve ratio will create five twists in the line every time the handle is turned.

A badly twisted line tends to bird's nest and is difficult to cast. Some twist can be eliminated by first removing all terminal tackle and then trolling the line behind the boat at high speeds. But a severely twisted line is hopeless and should be thrown away.

Improper spooling. For best casting results, the reel spool should be almost full of line—but not too full. On spinning reels, for example, a line will not cast properly if it only half fills the spool because too much friction will be created when the line goes over the top edge of the spool. On the other hand, if the spool is too full, the line tends to come off in coils, causing bird's nests. Most spinning reels should be filled to ⅛ inch from the top—but follow the manufacturer's instructions.

For best casting results with spinning reels, one should more or less match the line to the reel spool. Heavy line will not work properly on a small-diameter spool, and very light line will not spring properly from large-diameter spools. In other words, don't put 20-pound line on an ultralight rig or 4-pound line on a surfing reel.

Putting a new line on improperly can cause a degree of twist. This can be avoided by winding the line onto the reel the same way it comes off the spool.

I use one knot for 95 percent of all my bass fishing with monofilament line. It is the clinch knot, which, if properly tied, retains from 90 to 100 percent of the line's strength. Some other knots, by comparison, reduce a line's strength by as much as 50 percent. But the basic clinch knot tends to slip with some lines, so I use the improved clinch knot. To tie this knot, run a couple of inches of line through the eyelet, as shown in Figure 3. Then bend the end over and wrap it five times around the rest of the line, as shown in Figure 4. Next, run the end back through the loop formed at the eyelet, as shown in Figure 5. Finally, run the end back through the loop that was formed by completing the previous step, as shown in Figure 6. When draw-

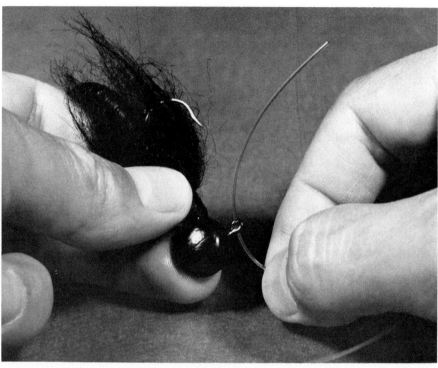

Figure 3

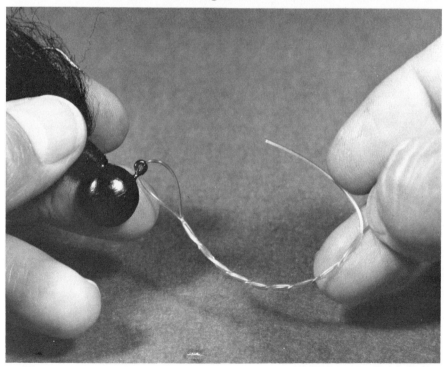

Figure 4

Figure 5

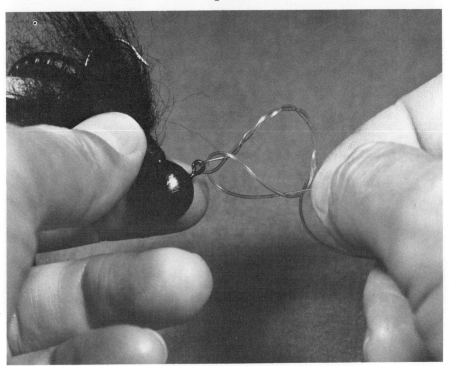

Figure 6

ing the knot down, I hold the line in my left hand and the lure (or hook) in my right. While applying pressure slowly and steadily from both directions, I hold the loose end between my teeth and keep it tight. After the knot is drawn down, I test it for strength and slippage. If it seems all right, I trim the loose end close with nail clippers.

When tying this knot, some anglers make a double loop through the eyelet, and others use a double strand of line. Either method complicates the tying of the knot without adding appreciable strength. Personally, I prefer to have a perfect knot than to have a double loop or a double strand.

It is very important when tying the clinch knot to wrap the line five times. Using only four turns can reduce the knot's strength by as much as 20 percent, and using more than five turns makes it difficult to draw the knot down properly.

Figure 7 shows an improved clinch knot tied with 2-pound Stren onto a No. 12 hook, enlarged sixty times through a scanning electron microscope. The stress distribution is difficult to explain, even when you see the distortion in the line at this extreme magnification. Here's what Du Pont says about its high-speed motion-picture studies: "They showed that properly

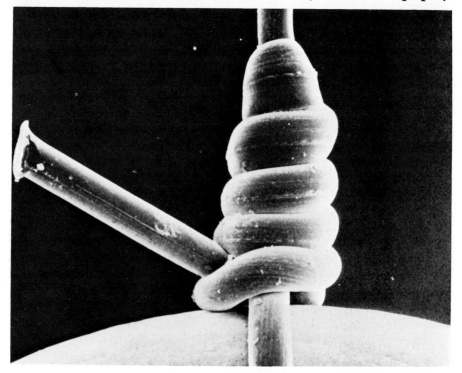

Figure 7

tied knots break at the very edge, where the last turn of the knot is wrapped around the center monofilament. Poorly tied knots tend to break in the center because the knot slips slightly and allows the total load to be carried by only one turn of the monofilament. The knot at that instant acts very much like an overhand knot and prematurely fails. Properly tied 5-turn knots distribute the load evenly over the entire length of the knot."

The improved clinch knot has been around for some time and is still widely used on monofilament. The newer Palomar knot, which is said to be just as strong as the clinch and easier to tie on hooks and small lures, is gaining in popularity. Personally, I haven't used this knot extensively simply because I get along fine with the improved clinch knot. The Palomar knot is tied as shown in Figures 8, 9, 10, and 11. Figure 12 shows the knot tied with 2-pound Stren onto a No. 12 hook, magnified sixty times.

The improved clinch and the Palomar are the only two knots that I recommend for tying monofilament line onto hooks, lures, and such tackle as split rings and swivels. A few other knots are needed when fly fishing for bass, and these will be discussed in Chapter 18.

Monofilament line is almost always used for spinning and spin casting. In fact, the development of monofilament was really the big breakthrough in the development of spinning gear. But a good braided line works better on bait-casting outfits, and there have been some noteworthy improvements in braided lines during the past several years. Cortland's Micron, for example, has a very favorable strength-to-diameter ratio, and a number of other lines have been improved in this respect. Casting a modern 20-pound-test line is as easy as casting a 15-pound line made a few years ago. I've recently tested a new Teflon-coated braided line, and it is very, very smooth to cast. I've also tested a "braided monofilament" marketed by Pflueger, and it also casts very well.

For bait-casting ease, the main advantage of braided line over monofilament is that it is more limp. Another advantage is that braided line has less stretch. And dacron braided lines have less stretch than nylon. Tests made by Gudebrod indicate that a 20-pound weight will stretch certain monofilament line 20 percent, a braided nylon line 15 percent, and a braided dacron line 10 percent.

Since braided line definitely spools better on bait-casting reels, why don't more bassmen use it? The main reason is that it is (or we believe it to be) more visible than monofilament. Even so, I believe that many bait casters are missing a good thing by not using braided line at times. I like it for casting fast-moving lures—but I hasten to add that I much prefer monofilament for fishing plastic worms and other slow-moving baits.

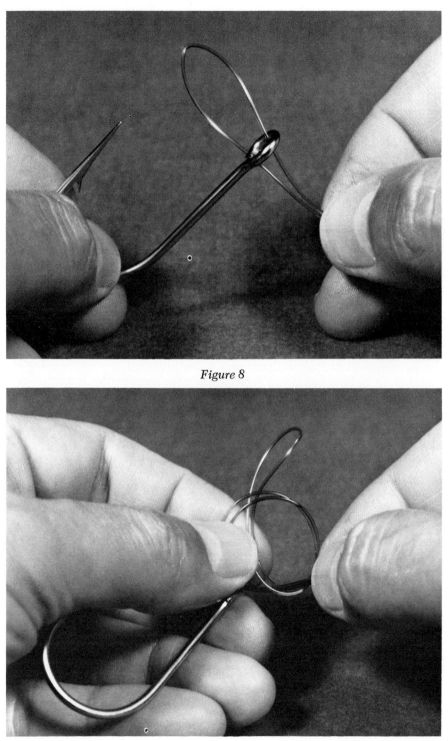

Figure 8

Figure 9

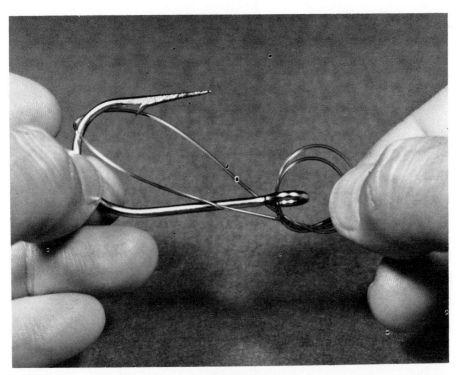

Figure 10

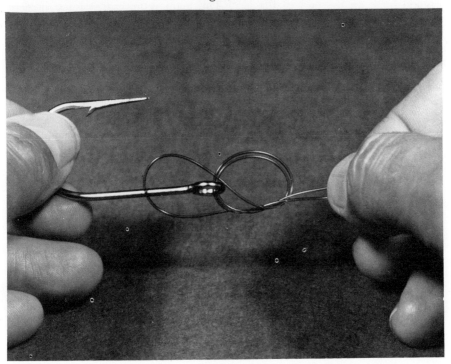

Figure 11

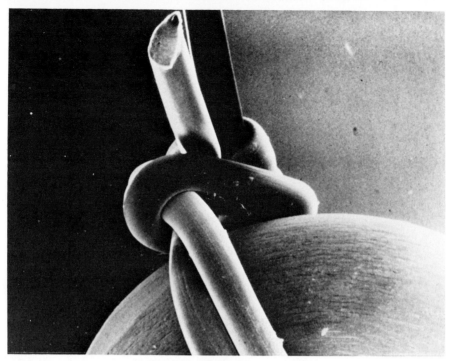

Figure 12

Gudebrod's brochure says that "the fishing line is the communication system between you and the fish." I like the thought, but I would add that steady communication is not likely to be established unless the angler has a good hook on the end of the line! The main requirement for a hook is that it be sharp. I always check the hooks on a lure—especially on a new one—before tying it onto my line, and a small Arkansas sharpening stone is a standard item in my tackle box. I also carry along a miniature file.

I prefer single-barb hooks to treble because I think they stick a fish better and hold it longer. They are also easier to sharpen. But a lot of artificial baits come with treble hooks, and I use them. I keep threatening to change them to single-barb hooks, but tampering with the hooks can upset the action and the balance of some lures. So, I usually fish with whatever hooks the manufacturer puts on the lures, but I'm not at all pleased with some of them. One of my favorite plugs comes with small wire treble hooks that are just too flimsy for some types of bass fishing. To be sure, they will hold the largest bass in open water if you have a dependable drag on the reel, but they are not always strong enough to horse a 14-pounder out of a submerged treetop.

I prefer the larger hooks for bass, but they are more difficult to set properly. The larger the hook, the farther it must penetrate to cover the barb; and the larger the bass, the tougher its mouth. So, if you're after a lunker bass with a large hook, the point had better be very, very sharp and had better be set with authority.

2

Rod and Reel

IF I COULD USE ONLY ONE REEL for bass fishing, my choice would be a free-spooling, ball-bearing casting reel with a good star drag. If I could have a second reel, it would be another free-spooling, ball-bearing casting reel with a good star drag. More specifically, I would want one to be a fast reel with a 5-to-1 retrieve ratio and a right-hand handle; the other, a slow reel with a 3½-to-1 retrieve ratio and a left-hand handle. The latter reel would be used primarily for fishing plastic worms and pork eels. If I could have a third reel, I would choose an open-faced, underslung spinning reel of top quality and medium size.

Well, actually, I would probably take a fly-fishing outfit as my second choice. But fly rodding for bass is almost a separate sport, and I have discussed the equipment at length in Chapter 18. I sometimes use a fly rod for bass because it's so much fun, although I wouldn't take one to a bass-fishing contest with $10,000 riding on every cast. The reason is that a lunker bass has a mouth as big as a gallon bucket and is more interested in full-grown frogs than in dainty mayflies. Nor is the limber fly rod ideal for horsing 12-pound bass out of treetops. But it's a great sport.

Personally, I have little use for those push-button spincast reels, although they currently dominate the tackle market, and many anglers fish with nothing else. Also, some expert bassmen fish only with open-faced spinning reels. I am certain, however, that most of today's bass experts, especially the tournament pros, rely mainly on good bait-casting rigs.

Here are what I consider to be the advantages and disadvantages of each type of reel:

Bait-casting reels. The better bait-casting reels of today (Figure 13) are far better than the older ones. The big difference in casting ease is that the gears can be disengaged for the cast. Only the spool and the line-guide mechanism move while casting, and some even have a stationary line guide; on the older models, all the gears and the handle turned. With modern reels, more distance is possible, lighter lures can be used, and backlash is all but eliminated in the hands of a competent caster.

The big advantage of bait-casting over spinning and spincast reels is that they are capable of greater accuracy, since the angler can "thumb" the spool while the lure is going out. By adjusting the thumb pressure, he can sit the lure down gently within inches of his target. With spincast reels, he has to push the button to stop the lure or bait, and it is likely

Figure 13

to stop quite suddenly, falling short of the mark and splashing down into the water. On some of the newer spincast reels, the angler can apply pressure gradually on the button. Still, there is no comparison between the push-button and the direct thumb contact. With spinning reels, which also cause abrupt stops and splashdowns if one flips the bail to stop the lure, it is possible to "feather" the line with one's forefinger while the lure is going out. Again, though, there is no comparison with direct thumb contact with the spool.

Most of the better free-spooling reels have a good star-drag system. This is of course invaluable in fighting a large fish, especially on lighter line. The handle of the reel does not turn in the reverse direction, which means that a bass can't jerk the reel handle out of the angler's hand and bust his knuckles. It also permits him to remove his hand from the reel handle to make adjustments to the drag even while the fish is running. Finally, the design permits the angler to override the drag by applying thumb pressure to the spool.

The big disadvantage of bait-casting reels, free-spooling or not, is that they are comparatively more difficult to use. Some people, including my wife, seem to have difficulty learning to cast properly. But the new free-spooling reels are much easier to use than the older designs, mainly because the backlash problem has been minimized.

Another disadvantage with bait-casting reels is that it is difficult to get much distance with the lighter lures. In fact, most bait-casting rod-and-reel combinations simply will not handle lures lighter than ¼ ounce, and some anglers have trouble even with ½-ounce lures.

Still another disadvantage is that the better bait-casting reels are more expensive than spinning or spincast reels. I haven't priced all the free-spooling reels on the market, but most of the better ones with ball bearings list at about $50 or $60. They are worth it to anyone who does a lot of bass fishing with artificial baits.

Spinning. Open-faced, underslung spinning reels (Figure 14) are a lot of fun, and I use them often, especially in open water. But, as I have already explained, they are not as accurate as bait-casting reels. They do, however, permit more distance, and they will handle lures as light as ⅟₁₆ ounce if they are properly spooled with the right weight line.

One advantage—at least to me—is that many open-faced spinning reels have interchangeable spools that can be switched in seconds. (My bait-casting reels also have interchangeable spools, but obviously they can't be switched as readily.) I usually keep three spools ready: one loaded with 20-pound monofilament, one with 14-pound, and one with 8-pound. (But the 20-pound stuff doesn't work too well and tends to spring off the spool in coils, causing bird's nests.)

Figure 14

The drags on open-faced spinning reels are generally good. One can override the drag by fingering the line as it comes off the spool, but this method is not as easy or as natural as thumbing the spool on a bait-casting reel.

Spincast. Push-button reels are very easy to cast with—if you aren't too particular about where your lure goes. As I said earlier, some of them can be braked on the cast, thereby permitting more accuracy and a more gentle splashdown.

The drags on the better reels seem to work smoothly enough for bass fishing, but there is no good way to override the drag on most models. The new Sabra reel (Figure 15), however, has an "automatic transmission." The drag on this reel doesn't work at all while you are turning the handle; if the fish makes a run, you merely remove your hand from the handle, and the drag takes over. If the fish is running into a brush pile or around a stump, engage the handle and you've got a direct pull on the fish without the drag being in use.

The larger reels, such as the big Zebco's, are quite adequate for bass fishing, especially in open water where pinpoint accuracy is not usually

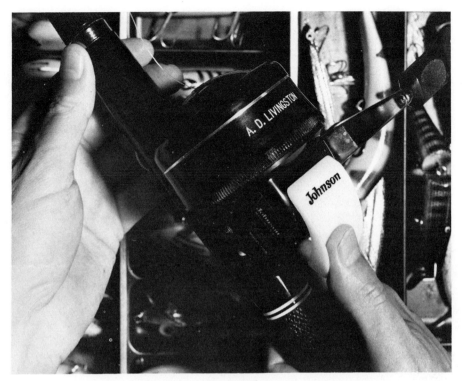

Figure 15

required. In addition to being easy to cast with, the better ones are virtually foul-proof. They don't have the backlash problem of bait-casting reels; nor are they as prone to bird's nests as the open-faced spinning reels, provided they are spooled with the right line. Still, they are just not accurate enough for the all-around bass fisherman, although I suppose some people do develop some proficiency with them.

Push-button spinning reels. I've recently been using a True Temper Uni-Spin rod-and-reel combination, as shown in Figure 16. Essentially, it combines the qualities of the open-faced, underslung spinning reel with the ease of the spincast reels. In other words, it's a push-button underslung outfit, with the release button extending up through the rod handle.

The reel has a unique drag system, which allows the pickup cup to revolve, instead of the spool, when the drag is working. Thus, you can turn the handle without twisting the line. The drag system also exerts a constant pressure regardless of how much line is on the reel. The reel seats into the rod, so that one has to purchase the whole outfit. It comes with three interchangeable rod tips in light, medium, and heavy action.

A spokesman from True Temper said that Uni-Spin was designed to

Figure 16

make all other fishing systems obsolete. Well, I like the outfit, and it could possibly replace my spinning and spincast reels, but I think I'll keep my bait-casting outfit for a while longer. And my fly rod.

Many lunker bass have been lost because the angler either neglected his drag or didn't understand it in the first place. Almost all modern drags make use of alternating hard and soft washers. The hard washers are usually metal, and the soft are some compressible material such as leather, felt, cork, or plastic. When an angler "tightens the drag," he is compressing the washers so that it takes more force to make them slip against each other; when he "loosens the drag," he relieves the compression. Even though selection of materials is important, and some materials work better than others for a particular reel design, I believe that most quality reels have adequate materials for bass fishing. It is important, however, that the washers stay in good shape, and they should be replaced every couple of years.

Actually, there are several kinds of drag exerted on a line in practical fishing conditions. There is a slow-speed drag and a high-speed drag. When a fish is running fast, the drag exerts more pressure on the line even though the setting remains the same. Another factor, sometimes called starting drag, is even more important for the bass fisherman; it is simply the force required to start the spool turning. Also, the friction of the line on the rod guides creates drag. The higher the rod is held, the greater this drag becomes. Rod drag together with the starting drag can be two or three times greater than the slow-speed drag the angler thinks he is using.

It's best to set the drag at no more than 25 percent of the line's strength. Sometimes one must increase the drag in order to turn a bass from a brush or treetop. This can be done in a now-or-never situation by making adjustments on the drag or, better, by thumbing the line. More drag can also be induced by raising the rod straight up. By the same token, the total drag can be reduced by lowering the rod tip. Indeed, knowledgeable anglers sometimes point the rod tip directly at the fish, eliminating virtually all rod drag! This is called "giving him the butt." I might add that some very good anglers would never point the tip at the fish because they don't understand the principle involved—or don't believe it.

During the past several years, I have broken two rods and have worn line-fraying grooves in rod tips long before they should have been grooved out. I also bought a new rod that had a faulty reel-seat mechanism. I returned the rod to the company and it was replaced, but the new one wasn't much better. The reel jumped out on me a couple of times, and it popped out just after my wife had hooked into an 8½-pound bass. Between the two of us we boated the bass, with me cranking the line onto the hand-held reel while she gained it hand over hand. After the battle was done, she said that she didn't want to use that rod again. I don't either.

At least potentially, the fiberglass rod is a great improvement over the old steel casting rods and is more durable than even the finest bamboo rods. But there is a lot of junk on the market—cheap guides and fittings, Mickey Mouse reel seats, and imperfect rod blanks. Some of the cheap rods don't have good action, or else they aren't balanced properly. The better fiberglass rods, on the other hand, have good hard guides and tips, and the tubular walls of the blanks are of constant diameter and uniform strength.

For casting or spin casting, I prefer a 5½-foot fiberglass rod; for spinning, a 6- or 6½-foot fiberglass rod. My choice for both is a medium-heavy action, but I also like to have a lighter 6-foot rod for us with 6- or 8-pound-test monofilament and tiny lures. For fishing with large shiners (discussed in Part Four), I prefer a light saltwater spinning rig.

A good many bass anglers are now using very stiff "worm rods." I own one, and sometimes use it, but these things are too stiff to suit me. It's difficult to cast with them. Instead of casting with a flick of the wrist, I have to sling the lure out. In just a few years, worm fishermen have gone from very limber rods to very stiff ones, and I feel that more and more anglers will swing back to a medium-heavy action.

There have been some interesting developments in rods and hardware during the past few years. These developments are discussed below, along with some related topics:

Ferrules. At one time, the ferrules in two- or three-piece rods were all made of metal; now glass-to-glass ferrules are being used on many of the better rods. They give the rod continuous action from tip to butt. Even so, the angler shopping for a new rod should consider one-piece blanks, unless he plans to do a lot of traveling about and therefore needs a break-apart rod. One-piece rods are better, stronger, and cheaper.

Tips and guides. Worn rod tips and guides can cause excessive line wear. For this reason, I insist on having guides and tips made of very hard, smooth material. For a while the Carboloy tips were my favorites, but some of the newer materials may be better. The Fuji Hard Speed Rings, for example, are made of aluminum oxide and are very tough and smooth. They are quite light as compared to carbide; in fact, they are now being used on some fly rods instead of wire guides. Incidentally, these guides, or some of them, are made to slip onto the rod blank; this rather radical assembly technique does away with tedious wrapping and makes it quite easy to replace damaged guides.

Also, the Fenwick people are putting a ceramic guide and tip on their 1400 series Lunkerstiks. Interestingly, the guides are placed higher than normal in order to reduce friction caused by the line slapping against the rod during the cast.

In addition to new materials, some firms are coming out with noncircular guides. The Quick people, for example, are putting a "Polygon" guide on the Finessa rod series. The new shape is said to reduce friction and drag because the line touches the guide at only three "points" instead of 360 degrees as with round guides.

Reel seats. There are so many reel-seat designs these days that I haven't attempted to test them all or even study the mechanics of their operation.

My best advice to anyone shopping for a new rod is to put a reel onto it before paying for it. A reel should fit snugly, without wobbling about.

Grips. Most rods have cork grips. Although a good one is quite satisfactory and will give years of service, I have taken a fancy to the contour grips on my Lew Childre bait-casting rods and don't want to go back to a straight cork handle. Other firms, such as Eagle Claw, are making contour handles of cork or wood.

Some rods come with an optional butt cap, and accessory butt caps can be fitted to almost any rod that has a straight handle. I like them, provided they don't throw the rod out of balance. The butt cap makes the rod feel a bit more secure when doing battle with a lunker or when casting with sweaty hands. I've never thrown a rod and reel into the water, but I know people who have!

Graphite rods. The latest material for building fishing rods is high modulus graphite, a material developed at the Royal Aircraft Establishment and used in aerospace. This material is lighter and stronger than fiberglass; in fact, graphite rods are approximately 25 percent smaller in diameter and twice as strong. At this writing, the rods were not generally available, but reliable tests on prototype models made by Fenwick indicate that they handle a wider range of lures, are more sensitive to vibrations transmitted by the fishing line, and increase casting distance as well as accuracy because rod vibration (whip) is minimized.

Sounds great, but there's a catch. The stuff is expensive. Casting rods made from high modulus graphite will have to start at about $150, and they aren't expected to get much cheaper.

3

Bass Boats

THE BASIC PURPOSE OF A FISHING BOAT is to take the angler within casting range of the fish. Often a boat is not necessary and may even be undesirable. On a small stream or pond, one can at times fish more effectively from the bank or by wading. Even on large lakes one can often score better without a boat, either by wading or by using an inner tube fitted with a canvas saddle. On Lake George in early spring, for example, some of the more successful anglers use boats only to reach the shallow flats. Then they get off the boat and wade.

If a boat is required, a canoe or a johnboat will often be sufficient, especially on streams and small lakes. But most bassmen either have or want a highly specialized fishing rig known as the bass boat. It has evolved over the past twenty years, primarily in the South and Southwest, to suit the needs of fishing for bass in the large man-made impoundments. During the past few years, the bass-fishing tournaments held on impoundments, or rather the requirements of the tournament fisherman, have had a questionable influence on the design of bass boats.

Apart from the initial race from the starting line to the prime fishing waters, the bassman competing in a tournament doesn't want to waste his fishing time in getting from one hot spot to another. Consequently, the

38

These bass boats are racing for the hot spots in a fishing tournament held on Lake Mead, Nevada. The pros like big, powerful bass boats.

boats have become faster and faster, and their motors more and more powerful. Some bass boats take outboard motors up to 100 horsepower, and a few have inboard–outboard engines of 150 horsepower or more. The boats have also become wider and larger because many of the tournaments are held on huge impoundments, some of which are 100 miles long, and white-capping waters are not at all uncommon.

Although bass boats of various manufacture do have certain similarities in shape and design, the distinction is no longer as clear-cut as with the canoe or the johnboat. In my opinion, the bass boat depends as much on accessories as on hull and frame design, and the better boats are, in fact, designed to accommodate the accessories. A bass boat without a foot-controlled, bow-mounted electric motor simply would not be complete, and fishing in a tournament without such a motor would be a severe handicap. In any case, here are the requirements and characteristics of bass boats:

Pedestal seats. The distinguishing feature of bass boats is the presence of pedestal seats and the absence of slat seats running from one side to the other. Typically, the pedestal seats are mounted fore and aft, as shown in Figure 17. This arrangement allows the angler to swivel his seat 360 degrees. Since there are no cross seats, he can walk from one end of the boat to the other without having to step over anything. The swivel seats

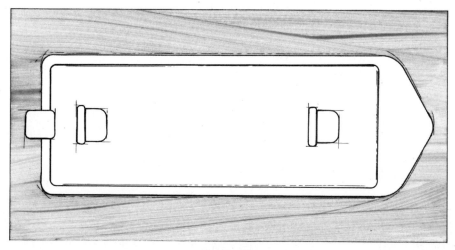

Figure 17

have a backrest, and a few models have armrests. They are both comfortable and functional for casting, since the angler can face in any direction without having to twist about. I prefer these seats for bass fishing for the same reason that a secretary prefers a typing chair to either a bench or a reclining easy chair.

But some manufacturers are, in my opinion, mounting the seats too high, as shown in Figure 18. (I quickly add that a good many bassmen obviously don't agree with me!) Although a high seat is desirable for fishing in deep water, it is not desirable in shallow, clear water because of the profile. High seats can also be dangerous.

One solution to the height problem is to install a seat that can be raised or lowered like a barber's chair. The Pro-Throne seat can be raised or lowered within a range of 10 inches. Thus, one can elevate the seat for fishing deep water and then lower it for fishing shallow water or for running at high speed.

Most of the swivel seats are molded from plastic, but some of the more deluxe models are foam-padded and have armrests. Some models tilt back as well as swivel. Even though some seats are more comfortable than others, the main feature of the swivel design is that the angler has more freedom of movement while he is casting or doing battle with a lunker bass.

One big advantage of swivel seats is that the angler doesn't get so tired when plugging for bass hour after hour. The result is that he will make more casts in a given length of time, and he will also be more alert because he'll be thinking about lunker bass instead of a backache. For these reasons, the average angler will catch more bass, especially on all-

Figure 18

day trips, with swivel seats on his boat than with slat seats. And he'll enjoy it more.

Electric motor. One of the most valuable pieces of gear on a bass boat is a foot-controlled electric motor, as shown in Figure 19. I would rank it above even the depth finder for my personal use, but tournament fishermen and others who must quickly learn a new lake would of course put the depth finder first. A foot-controlled motor is invaluable when you are plugging a bank or holding over, or near, structure. I find that, on the average, I can get in 50 percent more casts when I am using a foot-controlled electric instead of having to keep the boat in position by paddle

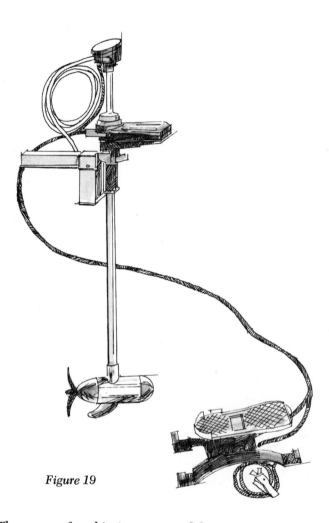

Figure 19

or oars. The reason for this increase in fishing time, of course, is that a foot-controlled motor leaves both hands free for casting and retrieving.

By comparison, the stern-mounted manually steered electric "trolling" motor is almost useless—at least to me. It makes the boat difficult to maneuver. The motor should be put on the bow, so that it pulls the boat instead of pushes it. Even a manual electric will work better on the bow. Ideally, the motor should be mounted front and center, but it works very well when mounted on either side of the bow.

By the way, anyone who owns a stern-mounted electric may hesitate to plunk down $150 or more for a new foot-controlled motor unit. I would like to point out that Shakespeare, Pflueger, and other firms market a foot-controlled attachment that can be used with most motors, and the unit can usually be mounted somewhere near the bow, as shown on the boat in Figure 20. I used an attachment for over a year, and it worked very well. The steering isn't as smooth as a Super Motor Guide, but it certainly beats paddling or rowing!

Some foot-controlled motors have only two forward speeds. Others have three, and still others have a rheostat control that permits infinite settings. Since the motors can be started and stopped with the foot, I have gotten along pretty well with only two speeds, but at times I have wished for a more precise setting.

Electrics are available in 6-, 12-, and 24-volt models. The 24-volt motors are nice if an angler needs them, but operating them with a 12-volt starter and generator system can cause problems. It's best to have a separate battery for the boat and two 12-volt batteries for the electric motor. But that's a lot of batteries for a small boat, and I think that most anglers can get along nicely with a 12-volt unit.

A new accessory called Weed Master is now available for motors with diameters of 2½, 3, and 3½ inches. It's a sort of ventilated funnel that fits over the motor, permitting it to go through weed beds. Grass, silt,

Figure 20

and fishing line can choke a motor down or, worse, can cut into the seal and cause severe damage.

The kicker. The size and design of the bass boat determines the ideal size of the main propulsion motor. I recommend that the angler use a motor of the maximum horsepower specified by the boat manufacturer. Often a smaller motor will not plane a boat properly, and a larger motor may be dangerous.

Steering and motor controls. There are three ways to control a motor on a bass boat. The simplest is to operate the motor directly from the rear seat. This method would normally be used with small motors having a manual start mechanism. Another arrangement, and one that is more common on bass boats, is to have a steering wheel and control console in front of one of the seats. The trouble with this arrangement is that it's difficult to cast and fish with a steering wheel in front of you. To avoid this difficulty, a lot of bass boats have a seat and steering console somewhere between the fore and aft fishing seats, as on the boat shown in Figure 21.

My favorite system has all the controls on either side of the front seat, which is a good place from which to operate the boat because one has a clear view of the water and can watch for obstructions. The arrange-

Figure 21

ment has a stick steering mechanism on the left gunwale and a speed control lever on the right. Thus, all controls are convenient for running but are out of the way for fishing. Another good feature of stick steering is that an angler fishing alone doesn't have to move from the front seat, since all controls, including the foot pedal for the electric, are within easy reach. The big disadvantage of stick steering is that it is dangerous when used with motors of more than 25 horsepower.

Floor plan. I've already touched on this topic, and the line drawing, Figure 17, shows a simplified floor plan. But a number of arrangements are possible, and the classic lines of a bass boat can be ruined by adding storage compartments, extra seats, live wells, and so on. While these are nice to have aboard (and some anglers insist on a live well), they tend to clutter the boat and hinder the angler's movement.

Hull design. Most of the fiberglass bass boats have some sort of cathedral hull. Typically, they have a relatively square bow. The design is quite stable, and walking in the better boats presents no problems.

Construction. Some of the bass boats are not put together as well as others. Bassmaster Grits Gresham has apparently looked into boat construction, and here's part of an article he published on the subject in the July/August 1973 issue of *BASSmaster* magazine:

> Two bass boat rigs on the dealer floor may look identical, yet one can be a safe, sound, excellent investment while the other can be exactly the opposite. In order to determine the difference, the buyer should approach his bass boat purchase with the intensity and dedication shown by auto buyers.
>
> The reliability and dependability of the marine dealer involved and the integrity of the boat manufacturer are two of the most important points to consider. Not only should the prospective buyer ask himself just what kind of a warranty the boat includes, but he should also determine the reliability of the dealer-manufacturer combination in standing behind the warranty.
>
> Production of fiberglass fishing boats is not an exact science, and workers on an assembly line are human. Even with the best manufacturers a boat will get through the inspection process now and then which does not live up to the specifications. If you as a buyer happen to get that particular boat, it is nice to get a satisfactory adjustment from the manufacturer—perhaps a new boat—rather than a "so sorry."
>
> The most inexpensive boat on the floor can be the most costly in the long run.
>
> Years ago a friend of mine bought a bass boat which looked almost identical to mine, but he quickly discovered that his "brand x" did not perform as well as he had been led to expect through fishing trips with

me. Not only did the boat fail to perform properly, but the bottom was so thin that in running in a chop of any size he could feel the bottom rippling beneath his feet. But the boat had cost him $200 less.

Another fisherman saved quite a bit of money on his bass rig, dropped it into Toledo Bend and let the hammer down. Less than half an hour later he hit a log running full bore and ripped the transom from the boat. His bargain rig went to the bottom.

The point is that the quality points of bass boat construction are usually hidden beneath the surface layer—out of sight. Some manufacturers have discovered, in fact, that they can hide gross defects in construction and workmanship by covering it with carpet.

The thickness of the glass in a bass boat hull is the principal determining factor in whether or not that stump you hit punches a hole right on through, and it is difficult for the average buyer to determine such a point except by investigating the track record of the manufacturer. The number of stringers and cross braces in the floor of the boat can vary tremendously, either contributing or not contributing to the rigidity and strength of the hull. Boats with insufficient stringer supports may perform beautifully when fresh from the molds, but after sitting on a trailer for a few weeks they tend to develop bottom hooks which destroy the planing capability of the craft.

Seat pedestals on some boats are screwed directly into the plywood of the floor, and in many cases these will pull free under unusual stress, such as when a hefty fisherman sets the hook. On others the pedestals are mounted on firmly placed blocks of wood which insure long-time freedom from trouble.

Does the boat have positive floatation in the floor? In some, the "floatation" is an air space between the floors—an air space which can easily be punctured. A good grade of foam injected between the floors is excellent floatation but provided that it is properly injected so as to reach all areas of the floor. In most cases this requires at least six or eight points of injection. Some manufacturers inject it in only two places, and that is where the foam remains. Yet that boat is advertised as having "foam floatation."

So . . . look around carefully, and closely, before paying a lot of money for a boat.

Anchors. A boat used for bass fishing needs two anchors, fore and aft, each with at least 30 feet of anchor line. Some anglers who fish deep impoundments may need 100 feet of anchor line. Although sometimes one anchor will be sufficient, the only way to keep a boat precisely oriented, especially in variable winds, is to use two anchors. I prefer mushroom-shaped anchors used in connection with a winch system. The anchors can be released by some sort of button or knob and can be cranked in easily.

The system keeps both anchor and rope neatly stored and out of the way.

Other features. In addition to electronic fishing aids (which are the topic of the next chapter), the more fancy bass boats have all manner of accessories and options. Of course, running lights are necessary for night operation and should be standard equipment. Nonstandard gear includes drink holders, cigarette lighters, stereo tape decks, CB radios . . . and who knows what else.

Along with the increase in size and horsepower, the price of bass boats has gone up and up. A fully rigged boat can easily cost from $5,000 to $6,000. That's fine for the anglers who can afford it. I quickly add that I can't, and a lot of other anglers can't either. In addition to the initial price of the rig, it costs more to maintain and operate a 100-horsepower rig than a 20-horsepower rig.

I don't believe that it's necessary to pay $5,000 for a bass boat, and I certainly don't believe that plunking out that much money will make a good bass angler out of a poor one. Day in and day out, the expert bass fisherman will catch more bass from a 10-foot johnboat than the novice will catch from the finest bass boat. But the big bass boats have certain very desirable features, many of which can be enjoyed on a less expensive basis. I have made what I believe to be a sensible choice in a bass boat, although it is a highly personal one and may not be the right choice for other anglers.

After looking at a lot of boats and their price tags, I settled for a 14-foot aluminum bass boat made by Fisher Marine. It is shown in Figure 20. Although most aluminum boats are too noisy to suit me, this one is surprisingly quiet, primarily because of flotation foam between the hull and the decking. My boat is light and doesn't require a large motor. Although most people would classify it as a johnboat, it doesn't have slat seats and therefore has to have a stronger hull and gunwales than an ordinary johnboat. In my opinion it's a true bass boat, and I actually prefer it to some of the larger fiberglass boats. It's fast enough to suit me, but if I fished in tournaments I would certainly want a larger boat with a powerful motor.

You don't have to have a "bass boat" in order to use and enjoy some accessories of the bass boat. A swivel seat can be mounted on slat seats, but freedom of movement is somewhat restricted; still, that back support makes a lot of difference during a hard day's fishing. A foot-controlled electric motor can be used on almost any boat, and it is certainly a worthwhile accessory. Sometimes mounting an electric will require a bit of modification, but something can usually be worked out. Some motors can be mounted fairly easily on most boats. I have a Motor Guide Porta-Pak, for example, that has a sort of universal clamp-on mounting system, so that I can use it with almost any johnboat, canoe, or rental boat.

I think, in short, that a poor man's bass boat will usually catch as many bass as a luxury boat and may sometimes catch more. But I have fished from those fancy boats, and I like them very much, and I plan to have a big one some day, red carpet and all.

4

Electronic Devices

ONE OF THE HOTTEST of the bass pros has said that his boat is primarily a platform for his depth finder. Indeed, the electronic depth finder is now standard gear on most bass boats, and fishing a large impoundment or a large natural lake without one would be a severe handicap for the new breed of bass anglers. Although the depth finder can be used to find fish—they are often called fish finders—most bassmen do not "hunt" bass with their unit. Instead, they look for likely bass habitats.

The depth finder is especially useful in "reading" a new or unfamiliar lake. With a little experience, the angler can determine not only the depth of the water but also whether the bottom is mud, rock, sand, or covered with underwater grass. He can spot drop-offs, submerged islands, old road-beds, creek channels, submerged timber, and so on.

There are several types of depth finders in use on bass boats, but all of them are sonar devices similar to those used on ships to spot submarines. The heart of the system, as used on bass boats, is a box containing the electronics and a calibrated dial. This box is connected by cable to a transducer, which is submerged. The arrangement is shown in Figure 22. The transducer emits sound waves, which in turn are reflected back from the bottom or from an object between top and bottom. The deeper the bot-

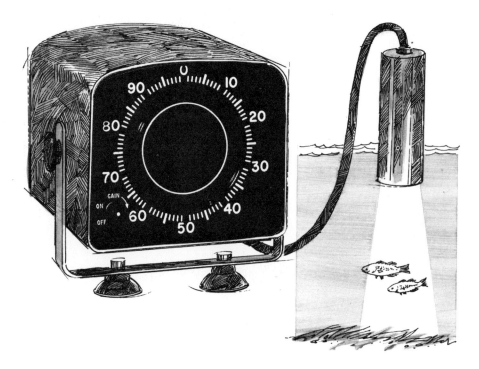

Figure 22

tom or submerged object, the longer it takes the signal to go down and "echo" back up. Thus, the time lapse is a function of depth. The unit measures the time lapse and shows a signal on a dial, which is calibrated in feet (or sometimes in fathoms). Note from the illustration that the transducer emits sound waves in a cone pattern, much like the beam of a flashlight. Any object outside this cone will not show up. Most cones are about 22 degrees.

Thanks to miniaturization and mass-production techniques, the sonar units are relatively inexpensive, at least as compared to the units used on warships. Most of the units used on bass boats cost from $140 to $180. What's more, they usually work and are surprisingly weatherproof. They are also more rugged than one might think. The better units have a "gain" control, which permits a sharp signal for various depths and conditions; they also have an interference suppression system designed to eliminate static caused by the boat's motor. Interference can be a real problem, especially with large motors.

Lowrance Electronics is probably the most popular manufacturer of depth finders for bass boats. The firm not only did the research necessary to produce an inexpensive sonar unit, but it also put on a good publicity

Electronic depth finders are standard equipment on most bass boats. This big Ouachita has two—one mounted on the left side of the bow and one in front of the steering wheel.

drive to sell the idea to anglers. Today there must be a dozen firms that make depth finders, and some of the larger tackle companies, as well as Sears Roebuck, are marketing their own units. And Heath Company markets a kit for do-it-yourselfers!

Anyhow, here are some of the more common types of depth finders in use today:

Flashers. The most popular depth finders have a circular dial and a neon light that indicate the depth, or depths. As explained in the Lowrance Fish Lo-K-Tor manual: "The transducer transmits sound waves into the water. At the same time, a high-intensity neon bulb whirls at constant speed behind the dial on a disc driven by an accurately governed motor. Although capable of firing 1000 times a second, the discharges are regulated to fire 24 times per second at zero on the dial. This gives a constant surface reading. But the bulb also fires 24 times per second at the point on the dial that indicates the depth, which is determined by the length of time it takes the sound waves to reach bottom and return. Although the bulb is firing at 24 times per second, it appears to the human eye as an almost constant light. In addition, echoes returned from any object in the water between the surface and the bottom fire the bulb too. Since these echoes are also timed, they show the exact depth of any fish—or any number of fish—in the water."

For example, the flasher used in the situation shown in Figure 23 would show red at 20 feet and at 35 feet. Clearly, the flasher units have the advantage of showing more than one depth. Because of multiple signals, width of signals, and intensity of signals, one can learn to differentiate, more or less, between various kinds of bottom. The next four figures, adapted from Jetco's Sea/Scope manual, show some typical situations. Figure 24 shows a hard bottom at 15 feet; Figure 25, a mud bottom; Figure 26, a rocky ledge; Figure 27, vegetation on bottom.

Getting the maximum use from a depth finder requires skill and practice. The first thing to do, of course, is to study the manufacturer's brochures and operation manual. The initial sessions with a flasher unit should, if possible, be on a lake one is familiar with.

Beepers. Most flasher units give only a visual signal. A few models, however, give both a visual and an audio signal. The audio devices can be set to beep at a certain depth. For example, let's say a unit is set for 10 feet. When the water is 10 feet deep or less, the unit beeps; when the water is over 10 feet deep, the unit is silent, unless a fish or some object happens to appear at 10 feet or less. Thus, the beeper/flasher unit can be used as a navigational aid or safety device, and of course it would also beep when a school of fish appeared at certain depths.

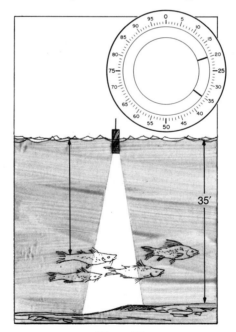

Figure 23

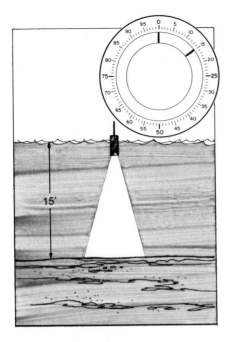

Figure 24

Figure 25

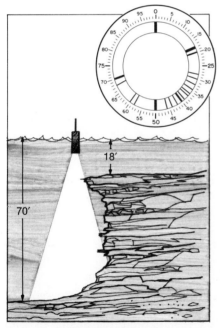

Figure 26

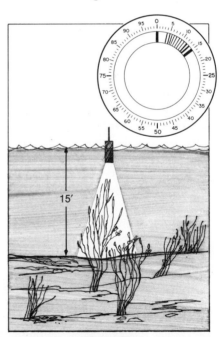

Figure 27

Recorders. These units actually make a record of the bottom and of the fish between top and bottom. Each unit has a stylus that continuously draws a line on a roll of paper. A straight line would indicate a smooth bottom with little or no variation in depth; a jagged line would show a rocky bottom; and so on. Although some firms are now marketing inexpensive recorder units, and combination recorder/flashers are beginning to appear, I don't think that recorders will ever catch on with bass anglers, or at least won't ever be as popular as the flashers. Storing all that paper tape can be a problem.

Mechanical dials. These units use a mechanical pointer instead of a light to indicate the depth. They are adequate for determining the depth, but they are not as good as flashers for studying the bottom in detail. The unit does not show multiple signals, although the pointer might oscillate crazily.

Portable units. Many depth finders have their own source of power. Usually they require two 6-volt lantern batteries. But a few models do use other types of batteries, such as D-cell flashlight batteries or transistor radio batteries.

Permanent mount units. These depth finders operate from a 12-volt power source outside the box. I prefer these to the portable units because I can operate them from the electric motor battery and therefore do not have to bother with changing dry-cell batteries from time to time. Usually, this type of unit has a gimbal mount and is attached more or less permanently to the boat.

Satellite units. A good many bassmen are using two depth finders on their boats, one fore and the other aft. Noting this trend, Fishmaster Products has come out with a flasher that has a plug-in satellite mechanical dial unit. Both units operate from the same battery and the same transducer.

The transducers marketed with depth finders are probably satisfactory, but some of the transducer mounts are not. Several mounts come with suction cups to hold the transducer to the side of the boat. I've never been able to get these to hold when the boat is moving at high speed, and they are generally a pain in the neck.

Several other transducer mounts clamp to the side of the boat or to the stern. Some of these are all right, but I distrust them for high-speed operation. Even if the clamp holds, the shaft may bend or break. There are, however, advantages in this type of mount. For one thing, they are portable and can be used on rental boats or on another angler's boat. Lowrance makes a neat clamp-on mount that permits the angler to scan all about under the water. The transducer can be angled from its normal straight-down position to a horizontal position, and it can be swiveled in a full circle.

Still, probably the best way to mount a transducer is to bolt it permanently to the boat's hull or transom. However, one has to be very careful about where the transducer is placed. It will not operate properly if air bubbles form under it, and this can be a severe problem, especially for high-speed operation. As a rule, air bubbles, caused by cavitation, are less of a problem when the transducer is mounted near the stern instead of near the bow. It is possible to mount the transducer underneath the boat or in a live well.

There is no doubt that the depth finder is the most important electronic device available to the bass angler. But there are several other devices that are helpful at times:

Light meters. A few years ago, temperature was generally believed to be the most important factor in a bass's choice of depth and habitat. But now light intensity is believed to be even more important. A bass has a fixed pupil, which means that it can't control the amount of light that goes to the retina. Nor can it blink or shut its eyes, because it doesn't have eyelids. Although a bass will feed in bright light at times, it prefers to lie in the shade of a log, mosey about under lily pads, or go deep where light doesn't penetrate as intensely.

The angle of the sun has a lot to do with light penetration, and so does wave movement, water clarity, and the cloudiness of the sky, as will be discussed in Chapter 27. The angler can learn from experience to adjust his strategy and tactics to allow for conditions that affect light penetration. Bassmen have known for many years that bass "bite better" on a cloudy or overcast day, and they have fished "on the shady side" of cover for generations. Today many anglers are putting all this common knowledge on a more scientific footing, and they have a gadget that measures the light intensity at various depths.

The meter is operated by lowering a sensor, or probe line, into the water and reading the "percent of light" on a dial. The probe line is coded every 5 feet, so that the angler can relate the percent of light to specific depths. Generally, the idea is that one should fish just below the depth at which measurable light penetration stops.

But note that bass can, and do, at times tolerate very intense light—when bedding, for example. Note also that bass in the shade of a log will rush out to feed in very bright water. The importance of light intensity should not be minimized, but I think it is more important for the bass angler to think in terms of cover, shade, water clarity, structure, and food availability rather than in lumens.

Temperature meters. Although temperature may not be quite the predominant influence that it was once believed to be, it is still very important. For one thing, it affects a bass's metabolic rate. Metabolism, in turn, influences how much a bass eats and how active it is. Temperature, then, has a bearing on what size lure one should use and on how fast it should be fished.

There are several brands of electronic temperature meters, priced at about $40. Usually hand-held, they are operated by lowering a sensor into the water and reading the temperature on a dial. The sensor is on a cable which is marked every foot so that the exact temperature can be determined at exact depths.

Another type of temperature device measures surface temperature. A sensor is mounted on the transom and is connected by a cable to a dial. The unit operates at high speeds, and, according to an advertisement, it "helps locate sub-surface conditions such as underwater springs, fresh water run-ins, currents, and thermoclines." I have never used a temperature meter of this type, but I do know that surface temperatures on a large lake can change considerably from one spot to another.

Oxygen meters. Like other creatures, a bass must have a certain amount of oxygen to live. The amount of oxygen in the water of a lake varies, depending on the amount of sunlight, decaying vegetation, and other factors. Some lakes develop a thermocline, especially in hot summer months, and may have one or more layers of water devoid of oxygen. If an angler fished in such a layer, he would of course be wasting his time.

The bass angler should be aware of the possibility of a thermocline and should know when and where one is likely to occur. A thermocline can be pinpointed with an electronic temperature meter, but the only easy way I know to measure the actual oxygen content of the water is to use a new meter developed for fishermen. As will be discussed more fully in Chapter 27, an oxygen deficiency may be independent of temperatures, so that the bassman who has everything else may want to invest in an oxygen monitor if he has any room left in his boat.

The first oxygen monitor, called the Sentry, was developed by Dr. Martin Venneman of Bass-Ox, Inc., and is now marketed by Ray Jefferson. Recently, Garcia has come out with a unit that measures both oxygen and temperature, and Waller is marketing one that measures light intensity as well as temperature and oxygen content. No doubt other models will be forthcoming.

5

Other Gear, Tackle, and Clothing

MY ADVICE TO ANY BASS ANGLER who plans to buy a new tackle box is to get the biggest one he can find. My first one was simply a cigar box. Then I bought a small metal box with trays, which served me well until I had too many lures and gadgets. So, I bought a larger box. And another even larger. After that, I bought a huge plastic box with two sets of foldout trays. It wasn't large enough, and a couple of years ago I invested in a big box with nine foldout trays and seventy-six lure compartments. This box also has two clamp-on "possum-belly" units that add 2,000 cubic inches of space.

In one possum-belly unit, I store reel oil, insect repellant, motor tools, a dozen jars of pork rind, and so on. The other (bottom) possum-belly unit contains my reels and extra line spools padded in foam rubber. More-over, I have two auxiliary clear plastic boxes, both of which fit beneath the foldout trays of the main box. One auxiliary box contains plastic worms, worm hooks, related sinkers, and jig heads; the other contains bass bugs, leader material, and other fly-rod gear.

When fully assembled, this double possum-belly box stands 20 inches high and folds out to 36 inches. Would anyone believe that it's not large enough? To be honest, however, I have to say that I don't usually take the whole works out fishing. I normally leave the bottom unit at home or in the car at the boat landing after I have put my reels on rods. If I'm going out for an hour or two with the fly rod, all I need take along is the small plastic bug box. And often I'll go out bait casting with only three or four lures.

I don't really believe that every bass fisherman needs a double possum-belly box, but I do think he ought to get a box a size larger than he believes he could ever possibly need! I also recommend that he take a close look at the size of the tray compartments before he buys; some boxes work nicely for spinning lures but not for large bait-casting lures. I had one box, for example, that had no compartments large enough for 7-inch Rapala lures or 6-inch stick baits. The angler should also make sure that the box he plans to buy has compartments for plastic worms, and that the material is "worm proof." Some worms "melt" or "burn" some types of plastic. In point of fact, many of the modern boxes are designed with the worm fisherman in mind, and some are made especially for plastic worms and worming tackle.

Most of the modern boxes are made of plastic or aluminum. The better ones are lightweight but quite tough and resistant to oil, gas, and corrosive agents. The only problem I have had has been with plastic handles. I broke a handle recently on my double possum-belly box, but the manufacturer replaced it with a heavy-duty handle at no extra charge.

After figuring the cost of all the boxes I have owned in the past, I can say definitely that the angler ought to look around for awhile before buying. Even so, the angler who fishes for arctic grayling in Alaska, smallmouth bass in the Ozarks, largemouth bass in Texas, and bonefish in the Florida Keys isn't likely to find a single box that will suit all his needs. I almost hate to admit it, but I am thinking about buying yet another tackle box. I do some night fishing, and Old Pal makes a "night-lighter" box with clear plastic trays. I don't see how I can get along without one. According to the firm: "If you fish at night, this one's your saving light. Saves you from holding the flashlight with your teeth while searching for tackle in the dark. For evening, night, and early morning fishing convenience this box lights automatically. Four powerful bulbs mounted in clear plastic trays 'pipe' diffused light throughout the interior."

In addition to the night-lighter and the worm boxes, there are other specialized tackle boxes, such as a surf box with shoulder straps (and I've got to have one of those because I do some wade fishing for bass), a stream box with belt loops (absolutely essential), a combination seat-and-tackle box for bank fishermen, and a "library" unit with removable trays. One of the newest of the specialized boxes was designed to hold two dozen safety-pin spinner baits, which are hard to fit into conventional boxes. The new design keeps the spinner baits hanging up, which prevents the skirts from tangling and matting.

Regardless of what kind of box one uses, it should be kept dry. A large box can hold a considerable investment in lures; it's easy to get $500 worth of fishing plugs and other lures into a large box. Water—especially salt water—will rust hooks and eyelets. I usually leave my box open overnight after a fishing trip, and I wash it thoroughly with a garden hose after fishing in salt water.

Finally, I have some advice for anyone who has the wild notion of putting a tackle box into a dishwasher, thinking that it will come out dry and sparkling like new. Don't do it. Just take my word on this—and don't ask how I know.

Landing nets. I seldom use a landing net because I believe that I have a better chance of boating a lunker bass without one. With bass under 4 pounds, I lift them into the boat with the rod (unless I'm using ultralight spinning gear or a fly rod). With a bass over 4 pounds, I grasp the lower jaw with thumb and forefinger (thumb inside). After I get a firm grip, I lay the rod down and slide my free hand under the lunker's belly before lifting it into the boat. Pressure under the belly partly paralyzes the fish so that it will not thrash about, which can be dangerous if it has taken a plug with treble hooks dangling all over it.

If there is a landing net in the boat, I prefer to use it myself rather than have some excited companion trying to scoop my fish up. If another person does handle the net, he should hold it *still* and let whoever has the rod lead the bass over the net.

Most of the landing nets that I've seen anglers take fishing are far too small for lunker bass. In my opinion, a net having a ring less than 30 inches in diameter is more a hazard than an aid in landing lunker bass. The rather large net shown in Figure 28 is really too small for bass.

In addition to a large net, I recommend one with wide nylon mesh (1-inch mesh will do). I also recommend one colored green or brown simply because a white net can frighten a bass into one last lunge—and big fish are hard to handle right at the boat. Remember that it's a mistake to take in too much line when landing a fish; keep the rod up so that there are 3 or 4 feet of line between the rod tip and the bass, as shown in Figure 29.

Buoy markers. Usually sold in sets of six, buoy markers often come in handy for marking a hot spot or for laying out a trolling route. There are two types. One is flat and works on the principle shown in Figure 30. The other is shaped like a miniature dumbbell. I prefer the flat

Figure 28

Figure 29

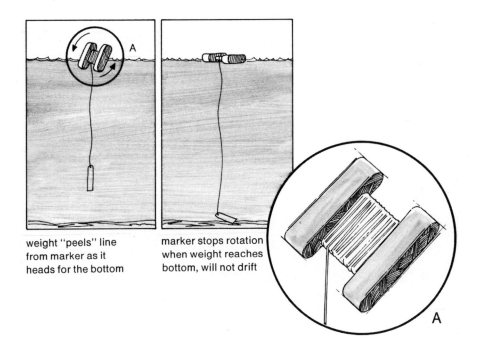

weight "peels" line
from marker as it
heads for the bottom

marker stops rotation
when weight reaches
bottom, will not drift

A

Figure 30

kind because they are easier to wind up and because the weight is a sheet of lead, which folds over the line for easy storage.

Clothing. A good bassman wears jump suits while fishing, but any comfortable outfit will do. In my opinion, it's best to avoid white shirts and white hats. But I may be wrong on this point. A one-year underwater photographic study of bass in Florida's popular Silver Springs indicated (according to Homer Circle's summary in the May 1974 *Sports Afield*) that an angler's clothing doesn't make any difference to bass. This study is available as a film documentary from Shakespeare, and I'm sure that it's worthwhile. Still, I feel that those bass at Silver Springs have seen an awful lot of tourists and very few hook-wielding anglers, since fishing is not allowed at the attraction. In short, I'll still avoid white or other bright hats and shirts, especially when I'm fishing in shallow water at remote spots that aren't used for pleasure boating, swimming, and water skiing.

It's wise to pack along a good rain outfit, especially on all-day trips. I prefer a parka-type rain suit as opposed to a raincoat. A poncho is a bit bulky to suit me, but it certainly will keep one dry.

Sunglasses. A good pair of polarized sunglasses is definitely an asset in bass fishing. In addition to cutting the glare and relieving the strain on the eyes, polarized sunglasses allow the angler to see beneath the surface of the water better than with the naked eye. This aids the angler in watching his line and in spotting fish that follow a lure in without striking it. (If this happens often, it indicates that something is wrong and the angler should vary his retrieve, change lures, or use a lighter line.)

Life preservers and safety aids. Never buy a life jacket or flotation seat that isn't approved by the U.S. Coast Guard. I prefer flotation seats, or cushions, for fishing, but it's a good idea to use life jackets or life vests when fishing on large impoundments or large natural lakes. Flotation jackets are available for cold-weather fishing, but I prefer a life vest worn over a sweater or windbreaker. In any case, and whatever your preference might be, *wear* a life preserver while you are fishing at night instead of keeping it stored under the boat seat.

First-aid kits don't take up much room and are sometimes badly needed. Buy a good one.

The Coast Guard recommends that boaters carry distress signals. Red-flare kits are available, and some kits also have orange smoke flares (for daytime use) and a distress flag. A good compass may also come in handy one day—or night.

Fish stringers. While baby sitting one afternoon, I decided to fish awhile from our lakeside patio, although I never expected to catch anything in my backyard. When I tied into something large and bulldoggish, I thought I had a big mud (bowfin), but soon it surfaced and I saw that it was a lunker bass. The baby, meanwhile, had made away around the house, so I more or less horsed the bass in. I put it for safe keeping into a large live box I had built.

When my wife returned from town, she was amazed at the catch. One of the neighbors came over with some old scales, which showed the bass to weigh about 11¼ pounds. But I felt that the fish was larger than that. I'm certain it was—I've caught dozens of big bass, and I knew this one was a real lunker. I would have taken the bass across the lake to a store that had accurate scales, but I decided to wait until I had taken some photographs of it. As it happened, a friend of mine and his wife were coming to visit with us for a day or two, and I knew that he would be happy to help me with the photos. So, I put the lunker back into the live box.

When my friend and his wife came the next afternoon, we set up tripod and camera on the patio, looking out on the lake. We planned to take the bass out in the boat, and my wife was going to shoot the pictures. I got the bass out of the live box and into the boat. Meanwhile, my friend had gone into the house to change his clothes and maybe to comb his hair. He stayed so long that I decided the bass had better be put back into the water so that it would look lively. I hooked it carefully through the lower lip with a safety-pin stringer. The lunker quickly took up the slack in the stringer, rolled over, and leisurely swam away! He had spread the safety pin open. That's one big bass that got away after having been caught for twenty-four hours! Anyhow, from that time on I have been reluctant to use safety-pin stringers on any lunker bass that I want to keep.

Another objection I have to safety-pin stringers is that most of them are metal (some are nylon or plastic, but I surely wouldn't trust a lunker to those, although they may in fact be quite strong). Metal stringers clank about in and against the boat. I've always felt that when I catch a large bass there may be others nearby, and I don't want to spook them with metallic noises, which carry for long distances in the water.

I usually use an ordinary 39-cent nylon panfish stringer. I've never had a bass break loose from such a cheap stringer, although one fish did jerk one out of my hand and take it off into the lake. If I ever catch what I believe to be a world's record bass, however, I certainly will not want him on a 39-cent stringer. I think I'll put him on the anchor rope. Twice.

Part Two

Fishing
the
Plastic Worm

6

Choosing a Worm

BASS FISHERMEN LAUGHED AT PLASTIC WORMS when they started appearing in tackle shops during the early 1950's. They were bought mostly as gags. But today they are no joke and haven't been for some time. They have, in fact, helped revolutionize bass fishing. More than any other lure, the plastic worm started bassmen fishing slow and deep, and it has influenced the design of tackle boxes, fishing lines, and rods. Beyond doubt, the plastic worm is the greatest bass catcher ever devised. Some very successful bassmen fish with nothing else.

Seasoned anglers have their favorite worms, but newcomers to the sport are likely to be confused by the infinite variety. Here are some points to consider when choosing a worm:

Size. Plastic worms are manufactured in all sizes, from 1-inch fly rodders to 18-inch lunker baits. It is entirely probable that the 18-inch worms were first made as a joke, but they catch big bass and are currently in demand in some parts of the country. The most popular sizes, however, are the 6-, 8-, and 9-inchers.

Actually, the size of the worm is not always entirely arbitrary and is often determined by the weight of one's line. With ultralight spinning gear, a 6-inch worm casts nicely without weight. With 20-pound line on

67

a casting rig, a fisherman must use a 9- or 10-inch worm, or apply weight, if he expects any distance on the cast.

Although I tend to use larger worms, from 9 to 12 inches, I firmly believe that how the worm is fished is more important than its size. Still, I hold that a 12-inch worm properly presented is more likely to tempt a lunker bass (especially a largemouth) than a similarly presented 6-inch worm.

Color. When plastic worms first became popular, black was the favorite color. Then red, purple, and other colors came along. Today the angler can purchase worms in every color and shade. He can obtain two-toned worms, striped worms, and spotted worms. Moreover, the colors are available in phosphorescent and translucent shades. One manufacturer, Stembridge Products, is offering a clear worm and felt-tip markers for do-it-yourselfers, and Cordell Tackle is marketing a "chameleon" worm, which more or less takes on the color of its surroundings.

Black and purple (or blue) continue to be favorite colors among serious bass fishermen, but other colors will, at times, catch more fish. Last year, for example, I was fishing a canal around sunset. The bass, up to 7-pounders, were taking yellow worms on almost every cast, while two anglers nearby were fishing purple worms without too much success. At times I have been successful with green worms and with white; I have also been catching bass on the translucent worms. But if I could have only one color to fish day in and day out, I would choose black.

Density and buoyancy. In addition to having many choices in shape, size, and color, the bass angler has a choice in the weight and softness of the worm material. Some plastics used in worms are softer than others, and there are additives and special manufacturing processes to make the worms lighter or heavier. One of my favorite worms, for example, has a hard head and a soft body. The hard head holds a hook better than a soft one and doesn't tear as easily, whereas a soft body apparently feels better to a bass, so that he is less likely to spit it out.

In addition to hardness and softness, there is a matter of buoyancy. Some worms sink and others float. Although a few worms are made to be fished on top of the water, the main value of a floater is that the tail floats up while the head is weighted down either by the hook or by added weight. This makes a very tantalizing bait if the worm is fished very slowly on bottom, either with a steady retrieve or with short hops.

Flavor and scent. At the outset of worm manufacture, the plastic was impregnated with anise and other additives. The anise worked like a deodorant by neutralizing human scent left on the worm by the fisherman. Human perspiration contains an amino acid called serine, which apparently stinks mightily to bass. Some manufacturers add substances that are believed to attract bass. Exactly how important scent is has not been determined conclusively, but I for one always wash my hands before I tie on a plastic worm!

In any event, some worm manufacturers are taking the scent/smell thing seriously and are constantly experimenting with various additives. Some worm fishermen are also taking it very seriously. Some of them punch holes into their worms and soak them in secret solutions, and others are beginning to hang bits of shiner flesh or crayfish tails onto their hooks when rigging the worms. Believe it or not, I recently saw a catalog listing for a capsule containing dried blood. The capsule has a hole in it, and it is inserted into a worm. When wet, the dried blood will soften and the worm will "bleed"!

Although I certainly don't ignore scent and flavor, it is my opinion that scent is not as important in bass fishing as in catching bullheads. This will be discussed further in Chapter 10. Let me say here that scent and flavor are probably more important when one is bass fishing with worms than with faster-moving lures.

Visual attractors. Most of the worms sold today do not contain hooks and are rigged by the individual fisherman, as will be discussed in the next chapter. Some worms, however, are rigged with one or more snelled hooks, and some of these have a small spinner or two up front. These rigs will catch bass, but most serious anglers do not use them.

I have seen other gimmicks to alter the appearance of worms or to add a bit of flash. The Netcraft catalog, for example, lists a "diamond ring" that slips onto the worm's body, and Gladding's new Squirm Worm has a flexible spinner that spirals down along the body when the lure is moved.

Sound attractors. Little Beaver Manufacturing Company has come out with a small capsule that contains tiny metal balls. When moved, the balls produce a rattle which, the firm says, imitates the communicative sounds made by crayfish and freshwater shrimp. Called Rattler, it is inserted into the worm as shown in Figure 31. There are also rattler sinkers designed especially for use with plastic worms. These are discussed in the next chapter.

The first soft plastic worms, made by Nick Creme, a machinist from Dayton, Ohio, looked exactly like a night crawler. Before long, various manufacturers started flattening the tail for better action. Then they started making splittails, fishtails, and so on. Some designs retained the night-crawler rings, whereas others were smooth and sleek, and still others were

Figure 31

beaded or globular. Once manufacturers and fishermen realized that plastic worms didn't have to look like worms, they became so venturesome that the term "plastic worm" is misleading. Chimerical lures like the Daddy-O (a cross between a worm and a crayfish) and the Horny Critter (both shown in Figure 32) are beginning to appear.

Today there are dozens of soft plastic lures on the market that are not worms. Nick Creme himself, who is the largest manufacturer of soft plastic lures, currently makes a number of creatures as well as his original night crawler. Here are a few from his latest catalog: grubworm, corn

Figure 32

worm, weed worm, white maggot, catalpa worm, shrimp, sand crab, cray-fish (several sizes and models), hellgrammite, frogs (several), water dogs, grasshoppers, crickets, various eels, lizards—and even soft plastic salmon eggs. (Trout anglers who fish only with artificial lures should note that Creme now offers soft plastic corn!) All these lures will catch fish if properly presented, but of course some of them are not as good as plastic worms for bass.

At the present time, the soft plastic salamanders are quite popular in some bass quarters. They are rigged and fished pretty much like plastic worms. Grubs and soft plastic lures of similar shape are also popular, but they are usually fished on jigs, spoons, spinner baits, or some other lure.

Even "pork frogs" are now being offered in soft plastic material. One problem, however, is that these baits tear off the hook too easily since they are hooked straight through instead of being threaded on like worms. Plastic "pork lures" seem to work nicely and will no doubt take bass, but day in and day out I'll stick with my pork rinds until I'm convinced that the plastic ones will catch more bass. Somehow, I can't imagine a tackle box as being complete without half a dozen jars of pork rind!

7

Rigging the Worm

I WAS AWFULLY SURPRISED a few months ago when a fisherman came to my house with a new package of plastic worms and some hooks. Unbelievably, he didn't know how to hook the worm. They kept coming off, he said. I didn't ask how he had been rigging the worms, but the small size of his hook indicated that he had been sticking the hook in one side and out the other, either through the head or the body, instead of running the hook longitudinally down the worm's body. Although plastic worms will catch bass when they are merely hooked on, here are better ways to rig them:

Weedless hooks. Probably the most common rig is a weedless hook inserted into the worm, as shown in Figures 33 and 34. Start at the head and work the hook through the center of the worm. Knowing where to bring the point of the hook out so that the worm's head fits nicely against the hook eye is a feeling that one acquires with a little practice; at first, a rough measure can be made by sizing the hook against the worm.

A hump can be made by running the hook farther down the worm's body. I seldom use a hump, but many fishermen prefer it. My objection is that a hump tends to make the worm twist the line.

The weedless-hook rig works best with a fairly large hook because part

Figure 33

of the hook's gap is taken up by the worm. For 6-inch worms, I use a 3/0 hook; for 8-inch worms, 4/0; for 9-inch worms, 5/0. However, this rule is not always valid because some brands of 8-inch worms are fatter than others.

Some of the weed guards on weedless hooks are too stiff to suit me. While a stiff weed guard is more weedless, it also causes some strikes to be missed. The weed guard can be weakened by depressing it with your thumb. If it is weakened too much, some of the stiffness can be restored by pulling the weed guard up past its normal position. In other words,

Figure 34

simply bend the wire up or down to adjust the stiffness of the weed guard.

The Texas rig. Although I prefer a weedless hook for fishing unweighted worms, the Texas rig is more popular these days among expert wormsters. It's a weedless rig made with a nonweedless hook. Usually, a hook with a bent or modified shank is used. (These hooks, along with weedless hooks, are shown in Figure 35.) Because the hook eye can be completely buried in the worm, the Texas rig is ideal for fishing with slip sinkers immediately ahead of the worm.

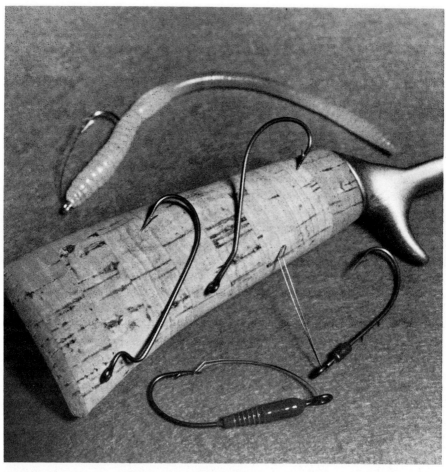

Figure 35

In the Texas rig, the barb of the hook is run in and out the worm's head, as shown in Figure 36. Next, the shank of the hook is run all the way through the worm's head; then the eye is turned over and embedded into the worm, as shown in Figure 37. Then the point of the hook is stuck into the worm's body, as shown in Figure 38, but does not penetrate all the way through.

Thus, the worm itself becomes a weed guard. When a fish takes the worm, however, the angler must strike back with enough force to pull the hook through the worm and into the bass's jaw. This rig works best with a stiff rod, a low-stretch line, a sharp hook, a very soft worm, and some muscle.

Most fishermen snip off the head to make the worm fit flush with a

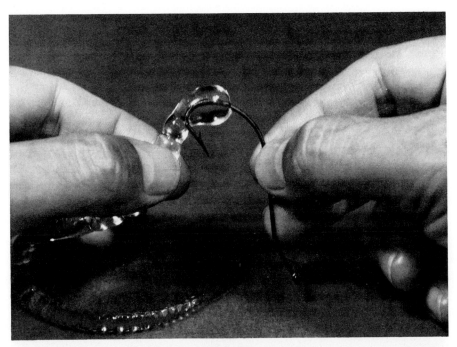

Figure 36

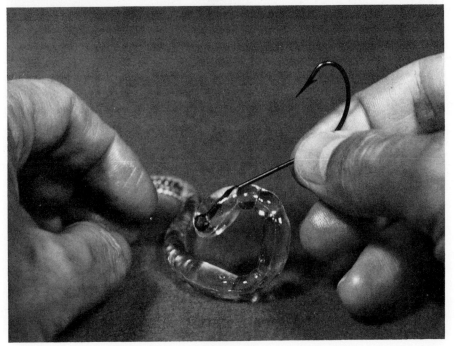

Figure 37

Figure 38

cone- or bullet-shaped sinker (to be discussed a little later). To help keep the worm from slipping, a round toothpick or wooden match stem is inserted through the worm and hook eye. The toothpick is then snipped flush. Purists, of course, use a colored toothpick to match the color of the worm.

The Texas rig, complete with slip sinker and toothpick, is shown in Figure 39. Clearly, it's a neat rig for use with a slip sinker.

Short strike rig. Some fishermen use a rig in which the hook is located not at the head of the worm but in the middle. This arrangement is made possible by threading the line through the worm with a needle, beginning at the middle and working the line out the head. The hook is tied to the line and embedded in the worm, as shown in Figure 40. The other end is tied to a swivel, which in turn is attached to the main line. The swivel is needed because the short strike rig tends to cause line twist. An alternate method is to thread the main line through the worm, beginning at the head and working the needle down the worm's body. Tie on the hook, force the

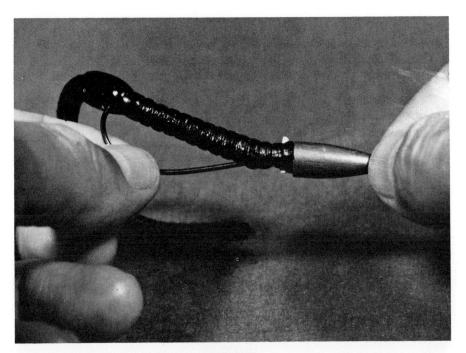

Figure 39

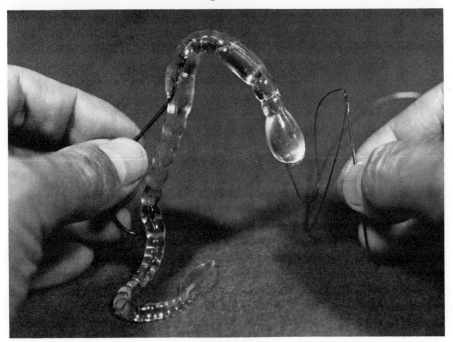

Figure 40

eye into the worm's body, and bury the point. Personally, I dislike any short strike rig. It alters a worm's action and causes line twist. And I doubt that it is any more effective in hooking a good-sized bass.

Snelled rigs. Some fishermen prefer to buy prerigged worms. Usually, they have two or three hooks and a spinner or two up front, as shown in Figure 41. The spinners, hooks, and snelling line alter the action of plastic worms, and most serious anglers avoid them. On the other hand, some very large bass have been taken on these rigs. A lunker that went over 13 pounds was recently taken in a bass tournament at Rodman Pool in Florida on a large, heavy-duty prerigged worm. It had snelled hooks but no front spinners or beads.

There are several methods of adding weight to a worm, and all of them work. The choice often depends to a large degree on how the worm is to be fished.

The hook itself adds some weight, often just enough to make a floating worm sink slowly. Indeed, many fishermen prefer that the worm sink slowly in shallow water. But a weight is certainly needed in deep water

Figure 41

so that the angler won't waste too much time waiting for the worm to sink. Weight is also needed, in shallow water as well as deep, when one is casting small worms with bait-casting rigs. In any case, here are the more common methods of weighting a worm:

Split shot. Pinch a split shot of suitable size onto the line about 12 inches above the worm. This rig is often used to fish floating worms near the bottom, and the distance from the bottom can be varied by moving the split shot up or down. Another method is to pinch a split shot onto the line right at the knot. This rig casts better than the first method.

Slip sinkers. Common egg-shaped slip sinkers are often used in front of the worm, either at the worm's head or up the line a bit. One big advantage of the slip sinker is that it allows the bass to mouth the worm and run with it without feeling the weight of the sinker. This also helps the fisherman tell when he is getting a bite.

Cone and bullet sinkers. These are slip sinkers designed especially for plastic-worm fishing. If the nose of the worm is snipped off, the cone sinker fits snugly, as shown in Figure 39. Some worms are now being made with flat noses so that they can be rigged Texas-style without any cutting. These sinkers and the Texas rig are very popular with bass fishermen.

Tunnel sinkers. These slip sinkers are recessed to fit over the head of the worm, as shown in Figure 42. They are available in different colors so that sinker and worm can be matched. The outer shell of these sinkers is made of plastic or some material other than lead.

Rattler sinkers. These are slip sinkers with loose weights inside a plastic shell. In addition to providing weight, they also produce a rattling sound that is supposed to attract bass. The first of these was the Rattleworm,

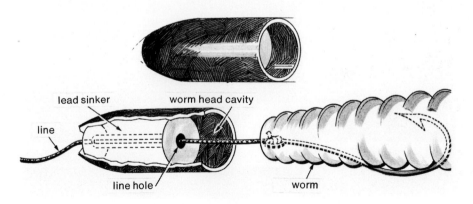

Figure 42

made by Captain Jim Strader of Tallahassee, and it has caught some real lunkers in Lake Jackson. The only other rattler sinker that I know about is Burke's new Rattlure, but it's a good bet that others will be on the market soon.

Spinner sinkers. The Eddie Pope Company has come up with a tunnel sinker that has a spinner up front. The spinner blade rotates while the rig is sinking as well as on the retrieve. The rear of the sinker is slightly dished out to accommodate worms with rounded heads. This is a nicely made piece of gear, and the spinner works.

Whisker sinkers. Cordell markets a sinker with a built-in bucktail. It works well with either weedless hooks or the Texas rig. As shown in Figure 43, the bucktail hides the hook eye, so that there is no need to bury the hook into the worm. I like to use whisker sinkers with 6-inch worms, jigging them along relatively fast or hopping them along the bottom. I often use a nonweedless hook with this rig, and I also use pork eels as well as plastic worms with it. By the way, some anglers are putting whiskers on plastic worms by threading rubber bands through the worm and then trimming the ends off.

Figure 43

Weighted hooks. Some weedless hooks have lead added to the shank. The lead is embedded into the worm so that the final appearance is exactly like the ordinary weedless-hook rig. The weight does cause the worm to bulge out and will sometimes cause a small worm to split. If they are properly rigged, however, the weighted hooks help make the worm stay put instead of sliding down the shank. I like the weighted-hook rig, and I use it whenever I want a little more weight for casting or want to take the worm down faster. It fills a gap between the nonweighted weedless-hook rig and the heavy slip-sinker Texas rig.

8

Fishing the Worm

I'VE SNAKED WORMS across the surface. I've inched them ever so slowly and steadily along the bottom, over submerged logs, and through brush. I've twitched them along at various depths. I've jigged and bumped them along the bottom with minute hops, and I've pumped them in with long upward sweeps of the rod. I've dangled their tails from lily pads, and I've held them suspended above the water from brush. I've fished them weighted and unweighted. I've rigged them with weedless hooks, and I've used the Texas rig. I've tried this color and that, and I've fished with all sizes up to 18 inches long. My conclusion is that it's difficult to miss with plastic worms, provided that they are fished near bass that have not been spooked. But this does not mean that one fishing technique is as good as another, one color as good as another, or one rig as good as another. Nor does it mean that a poor fisherman can catch as many bass as a good fisherman, even when both of them are using the same worm, rig, and fishing technique from the same boat.

Although many successful wormsters rig and fish pretty much the same way all the time, I feel that versatility will help most anglers catch more bass. Personally, I vary my rig and technique to suit the kind of water I'm fishing in, bearing in mind the time of day and the season of the year.

A good deal depends on whether I'm fishing in shallow water or deep.

Fishing shallow water. In water from 2 to 6 feet deep I do not normally use a slip sinker or any other kind of weight. I want the worm to sink down slowly. Many of the strikes come while the worm is going down, so I keep a very, very close eye on the line. A twitch or a faster sinking rate could mean that a bass has taken the worm. After it sinks to the bottom, I let it rest for a few seconds and then twitch it along with short jerks. If this tactic doesn't work, I'll speed up my retrieve—or slow it down. At times, a slow, steady retrieve will work better than any other, especially on an uneven bottom.

Note that an unweighted worm has a different action from a weighted worm. When twitched, it will dart about more from side to side, whereas a weighted worm has more up-and-down motion. The up-and-down motion may be better in some cases, and it's a fact that many very successful bass anglers always use a slip sinker in shallow water as well as deep. I suspect, however, that the weight is used more as an aid in casting than as a device to impart more up-and-down motion to the worm.

Fishing worms without a weight can severely limit one's casting distance, which can be important in shallow, clear water. It's difficult, for example, to get much distance with a 6-inch worm when one is using a 20-pound line and a bait-casting outfit. The solution to the problem is to use either a larger worm or a lighter line. I usually fish an unweighted worm on a spinning rig spooled with 8-pound line. But if I'm after a real lunker, I use a 12-inch worm on a casting outfit spooled with 20-pound line. Day in and day out, though, light line on a spinning rig will catch more pounds of bass. One reason is that the line is less visible, and another reason is that light line is more limp than heavy line, thereby giving the worm a different action.

I might also add that not all brands of worms are equally suited for fishing without weights. The action is different, either because of the shape of the worm or because of the plastic formula from which it was made. I especially like the Bagley spring tail and the Cordell pencil worm for fishing without weights.

One technique that sometimes works in shallow water is to work an unweighted worm fast, either snaking it on top or twitching it along just under the surface. This method presents a problem to some fishermen who let a bass run with a worm before they set the hook. Their immediate reaction is to strike back when a bass hits a fast-moving worm, but they check this reaction and give slack—often after sticking the bass just enough to spook it. The correct procedure is definitely to set the hook immediately and hard.

When I do use a weighted worm of one sort or another in shallow water, I usually prefer one with a high-floating tail. I pull it along with a start/stop motion, often with hops of only an inch or two. This keeps the head down and imparts a teasing motion to the tail, which of course floats upward. If this tactic doesn't work, I retrieve the worm with long overhead sweeps of the rod tip, pausing four or five seconds between each sweep.

Fishing deep water. I seldom fish an unweighted worm in water deeper than 8 feet. The reason is simply that it takes an unweighted worm too long to sink down, thereby wasting fishing time. I sometimes use a weighted weedless hook in water from 8 to 15 feet deep. The weighted hook takes the worm down fast enough, and I believe it looks more appealing while it sinks than a worm rigged with a heavy slip sinker.

This South Dakota bass is trying to shake a large plastic worm.

In water deeper than 15 feet, a slip sinker is definitely called for, and of course the slip sinker works best with the Texas rig. After casting a heavily weighted worm into deep water, I keep a tight line while it is going down. If it gets to the bottom without a strike, I let it lie there for a few seconds. Then I retrieve it by short hops or long sweeps. Generally, I try to make the hops and sweeps slower than when I am making similar retrieves in shallow water.

One point to consider when you are fishing deep water is where your lure is going to be when it hits bottom. If you keep a tight line, the lure won't fall straight down; instead, it will fall in an arc. Obviously, a 50-foot cast in 60 feet of water will not permit the lure to touch bottom, and it will end up directly under the boat. One solution to this problem is to strip off line fast while the lure is sinking, but this method makes it more difficult to detect that slight twitch made when a bass engulfs a free-falling bait. Another solution that often works is to make a longer cast. For example, you spot a limb of a tree sticking up in 30 feet of water and you think it might be part of an underwater brush pile. If you cast the worm directly at the stickup, it will arc away from the cover you want to fish out. So, cast beyond the stickup and let your worm arc into the cover.

Fishing in deep water generally is more difficult than fishing shallow. But if the angler masters the techniques (which are discussed more fully in Chapter 13), he'll catch more bass, and larger ones.

Fishing in cover and structure. These topics are discussed in Chapters 15 and 16, but let me say here that the plastic worm is ideal for fishing in grass, treetops, and other thick cover and structure. In addition to being very good bait, it is probably the most weedless of all lures.

Setting the hook. The real secret of catching bass on plastic worms is in detecting the "strike" and then setting the hook properly. As I've said, it is important to watch your line closely and to keep it tight so that the slightest bump will be felt. When you do feel a fish, immediately point your rod toward it and quickly take up the slack. If it's still there when the slack is out, strike back hard. I mean hard. There is a saying among bassmen that you have to set a hook as though you're trying to cross the bass's eyes. It's a good saying to remember.

There are several difficulties in setting a hook while worm fishing. First, the bait is usually moving slowly, or not at all, when the bass takes it. Second, the hook must be set either through the worm (Texas rig) or in spite of a weed guard. Third, the hook itself is large as compared to hooks on other lures of the same weight. Fourth, most worms are fished with monofilament, which has a good deal of stretch.

The worm fisherman will therefore profit by having a very sharp hook, a stiff rod, and a strong arm.

More and more anglers are using plastic worms in conjunction with other lures. And some new lures are being manufactured with worms attached. Here are some possibilities:

Spoon worms. I've been fishing 6-inch worms behind spoons for years, especially when I would find myself short of a suitable pork rind. Now the Johnson people (and possibly other manufacturers) have come out with a spoon worm, as shown in Figure 44. Actually, it is an ordinary Johnson spoon with the weed guard snipped off a bit; the worm is stuck onto the abbreviated weed guard and impaled on the hook. Uncle Josh, Cordell,

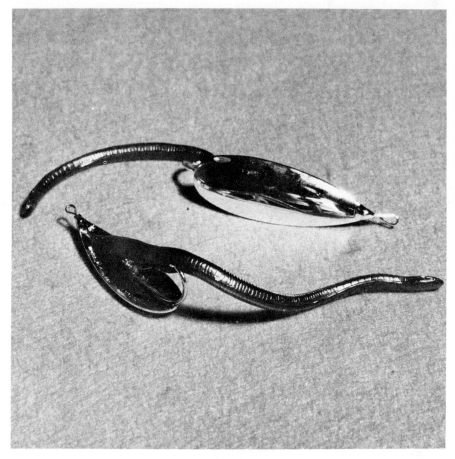

Figure 44

and other firms are making spoons designed especially for use with plastic worms and pork eels, as shown in Figure 45. These kicker spoons give a worm, or a pork eel, a good swimming action, and they are excellent for bumping bottom.

Jig worms. Special jig heads, some weedless, were being manufactured not long after the plastic worm became popular. They can be jigged at various depths or bumped along the bottom. Figure 46 shows Tony Accetta's Sneaky Pete jig worm together with Gapen's Hairy Worm Plus, an

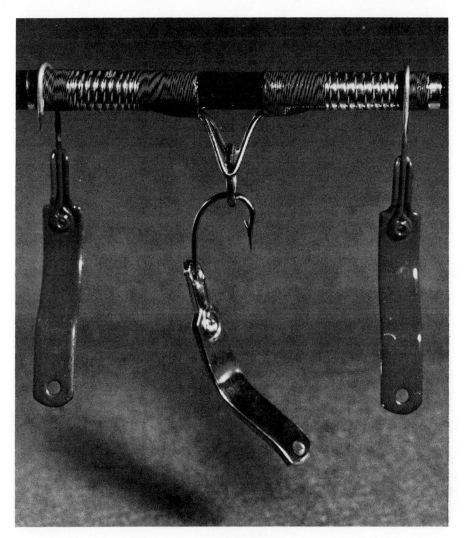

Figure 45

Figure 46

excellent safety-pin spinner and worm rig. Actually, 4- and 6-inch worms can be used effectively behind any spinner bait that has a single hook and a skirt or bucktail.

There are so many different types of worm, so many sizes, so many colors, and so many rigs that to cover them all and to master the nuances of fishing each would be impossible. Ten shapes, ten colors, and ten sizes would yield a thousand possible combinations. Add ten degrees of buoyancy and the possible combinations would be 10,000. I fear, therefore, that I have omitted some technique, such as holding your mouth a certain way when you impart that little twitch, that may take more bass with a certain worm rigged in a certain way and fished under certain conditions.

Many bassmen have some pet technique or gimmick, such as tying a knot in a worm, casting it out, and letting it untangle itself on the bottom. Others fish a worm so slowly that they average only a dozen casts an hour. Even though an ultraslow retrieve will catch bass, and some big ones, I think that a faster retrieve and more casts will catch more bass in the long run. It's a matter of playing the odds, and I believe that the worming techniques previously set forth will give the average angler the best chance of catching bass.

There are exceptions, and at times the novice fisherman will catch more bass than the more seasoned angler. Not long ago, for example, I took a man out fishing while his wife and little girl stayed home with my wife. We fished several hours with our sophisticated gear and didn't get a nibble. When we came in, the little girl had caught two bass just off our lakeside patio, using a $5.95 spincast outfit and old plastic worms. She had just slung the worms out into open water and waited. She imparted no action to the worms. After a while she would calmly turn to our wives and say, "I think I've got something."

I heard of one bluegill fisherman, who obviously didn't know what he was doing, who caught a 20-pound bass out of Lake Tarpon. He was fishing with a cane pole and merely slung the worm out and let it lie on the bottom!

I could, of course, say that the exceptions and freak catches only serve to prove the rule. But if that old saying makes any sense at all, I've never been able to puzzle it out. I think, however, that the exceptions do prove that it's difficult to fish a plastic worm wrong.

9

Outlaw the Worm?

DAY IN AND OUT, the soft plastic worm will catch more pounds of bass than any other lure or any live bait. About 90 percent of the bass caught in fishing tournaments are taken on plastic worms, although there are exceptions when hard plugs and spinner baits have taken the money. If I were a tournament fisherman, I would no more go out on an impoundment without a sackful of worms than I would go to a golf course without a good driving stick. Yet, there are some counts against the worm, and I know several dedicated bass anglers who refuse to fish with them.

First, the properly rigged, ultraweedless plastic worm is detrimental to the art of plug casting. The complete plugger takes pride in placing a gang-hooked lure within inches of a perilous treetop or stump. This is itself a sport with pluggers, and they can enjoy themselves regardless of whether or not they catch any fish. They like to cast accurately, and the worm takes the element of risk out of casting. Being ultraweedless, they can be slung right into felled treetops, overhanging brush, vines, and other places where a plug would hang up so badly that it would have to be unhooked by hand.

Consider how I fell into sloth. When plastic worms became the thing, I bought a spinning rig and for seven years fished with nothing else. Then I bought a superduper, free-spooling, ball-bearing bait-casting outfit, and I was surprised to learn that I couldn't place a plug accurately. Part of the problem was that I had gotten out of practice and had fallen into the habit of casting those worms almost with abandon. Instead of trying to place a worm into a pocket, I would overshoot the mark and then drag the worm back into fishing position. In short, worm fishing spoiled me, and I had to learn how to cast all over again.

Second, the plastic worm is usually fished slowly. The angler makes fewer casts with worms than with a spoon or plug or spinner bait. Some anglers dislike this. My brother-in-law, for example, says that he had just as soon anchor and fish with shiners or crawdads. He likes to plug a bank, and when I fish with him I hesitate to use plastic worms because they slow him down. I like to fish with him—I like it very much—but I'm certain that we would catch more bass (most of the time) if we would forget our casting and sling out some worms. But he won't, and I'll continue to fish with him.

Third, and much more important, the plastic worm gut-hooks too many small bass. For this reason I sometimes think the worm ought to be illegal. But it isn't and won't be, and I think it's up to the individual sportsman to avoid gut hooking small bass.

The big reason that so many small bass have been killed goes back to the early days of worm fishing. At that time most anglers were using light, limber spinning rods and 8-pound-test lines. This combination, together with the weedless hooks, made it difficult to set the hook unless the bass did swallow the worm. Hence, the practice of letting the bass run. But modern bassmen, armed with stiff rods, have learned to set the hook quickly, before a small bass swallows the worm or before a big one spits it out.

Another good reason for setting the hook quickly is that I, for one, don't want to gut-hook a very large bass. I feel that I would have a much better chance of weighing in a world's record largemouth if I hooked it through the corner of the mouth or some spot where it would chomp down on the hook instead of on my line. Those fine "teeth" can considerably weaken monofilament as well as braided line.

I've noticed during the past few years that more and more outdoor writers have started recommending that the angler set the hook quickly, which is definitely a shift from the "let him run" advice that was being given a few years back. I suspect that some of us have a guilty conscience about gut hooking so many small bass. I know I do, and I still gut-hook one occasionally.

Not long ago, for example, my wife announced that we were having guests that night and she would like to have a fish fry. But the freezer was empty, and I wasn't sure that I could come up with 10 pounds of bass on such short notice. Her suggestion that I pay good money for some grouper at the fish market, however, sent me off in a huff, and I almost broke the cord while cranking the outboard.

I headed for a canal where I thought some bass could be located. Before sundown, I caught four that would average about 2½ pounds each and one that was about 8 inches long. The small fish swallowed a pencil worm, and I felt that it would die if I released it. Since I wasn't quite certain that I had enough fish to feed everybody, I decided to string it up.

As usual, our four-year-old son met me at the boathouse and asked to see my catch. Being proud of my ability to bring home the meat, I held the stringer high. But he didn't marvel at the catch. Ignoring the four keepers, he pointed to the yearling and said, "That's the littlest bass I ever saw!"

Part Three

Fishing Spoons, Plugs, and Other Lures

10

Choosing a Lure

ALTHOUGH THE MANUFACTURERS are doing a great job on lure design, I am not happy with the results of mass production and modern packaging. When I pay $1.50 for a spinner bait, I want it to spin. When I pay $2.00 for a rattler lure, I want the thing to rattle. Before purchasing a lure, I like to take it out of the box and look at it and weigh it in my hand and shake it. But, unfortunately, many lure makers—even some of the better ones—are encasing their lures under plastic bubbles on display cards. There's no way to get at them without tearing up the packages. This may be a blessing for retailers, but I, for one, seldom buy these lures unless I am already familiar with them, for the same reason that I seldom buy a book in a bookstore without first browsing through it.

I am also unhappy with the hooks being sold on some lures. They are dull. I've noticed that one of my old favorites, a spoon, has become especially blunt. Most of the new ones are as dull as a kitchen fork. I wrote the manufacturer a letter of constructive criticism, explaining that the lure had for a long time been one of my favorites. I said that I was sure that the hook was so very dull because of the company's plating and lacquering processes. The marketing manager, or somebody with some such title, thanked me for my letter and said that some of the hooks were dull because

of the plating and lacquering processes; he hoped that the individual fisherman would sharpen the hooks before using them. Well, a fisherman should
not have to sharpen a new hook, but I almost always do. More important,
many anglers who buy that spoon don't know that they should sharpen it.
I've seen pluggers break out a new lure and tie it on without even checking the point of the hook. And checking the point isn't enough. Some
hooks on new lures have the barb completely choked up with paint.

At the very least, manufacturers should state somewhere on the package
that the lure may need sharpening. But of course they don't. In fact,
many manufacturers are not saying much of anything on their packages
these days. Some of them don't even state the weight of the lure.

Just the other day, a representative of a lure company told me that the
company had gotten a very good response from some instruction sheets
that it had started packaging with its lures. Although some firms do include such instructions, many don't, and some who once did provide instructions and fishing tips have dropped them. In no case that I know about
does a lure company publish *enough* information about its products. Some
of the modern lures, such as the safety-pin spinner baits, are very versatile
and can be fished in several ways. It would seem to me that manufacturers
would profit by publishing this information in detail, so that anglers would
catch more fish and purchase more lures of the same make.

While their published information is getting more and more sparse, most
manufacturers are, ironically, learning more and more about how their
lures behave. By using instrumented test tanks, they can study how fast a
lure sinks, how deep it runs, and other characteristics that ought to be
passed on to fishermen. Some manufacturers are studying how much light a
lure reflects and how much sonic vibration it emits. This information is
invaluable in lure design, especially when coupled with our increasing
knowledge of how vibrations and light reflection influence bass. I predict
that before many more years we will know so much about bass and lure
behavior that the large tackle firms will be using computers to design lures.
Maybe some of the larger ones already do. In any case, I would like to see
lure makers start publishing their data on sonic vibrations, reflectivity, and
so on.

In addition to studying lure behavior in test tanks, many manufacturers
are doing a lot of research with scented lures. With most animals, there is
a relationship between scent and taste, and with fish the two senses seem to
merge into one. I've already discussed in Part Two the scented and flavored
plastic worms. But the research is extending beyond the soft plastic lures.
Old Pal, for example, is now marketing several hard lures with a Hydron
porous plastic coating that releases scent when it is wet and seals it in when

dry. According to the firm, the scent lasts for approximately twenty hours of fishing and can be recharged from a spray can.

Izaak Walton mentioned scented baits in his *The Compleat Angler,* and he said that the Romans had used various stink baits to attract fish. Walton, however, didn't put much stock in scents. I think it depends a good deal on what sort of fish one is angling for. Some fish, such as the bullhead, no doubt feed primarily by the sense of taste/smell. Trout, on the other hand, feed primarily by sight and often on very small insects. But note that many a noble trout has fallen to a gob of cheese or a sweet kernel of fresh corn.

The author's brother-in-law chose a top-water rattler lure to fool this lunker.

Bass do not feed primarily by smell and taste, and I don't believe they rely on sight as much as a trout does. I doubt that a bass could see a No. 20 Ginger Quill from 3 feet away. I may be wrong, but I believe that a bass's main sense is one of "hearing" or feeling vibrations in the water. It hears with virtually its whole body, and the signals are amplified by a hollow bone structure. The lateral line on either side of the body is heavily concentrated with sound and vibration sensors. Because it has these lateral lines on *both* sides of its body, it can tell pretty much where a lure hits the water, its direction and its speed. Thus, bass can start hunting a plug even before they see it. I fully believe that a blind bass, aided by its huge mouth, can catch a plug.

I don't think anyone knows exactly how important scent is to a bass. I do, however, think it is reasonable to assume that a bass can sense a good-smelling lure—or a bad-smelling one. It is believed that bass are repelled by the smell of human hands and by such materials as reel oil and gasoline. For this reason, I try to remember to wash my hands in lake water before tying on a lure, especially one that is to be fished slowly. I'm not absolutely convinced that these precautions are necessary, but I don't take any chances. I understand that some anglers these days are dipping their lures in bourbon, which they believe to be a bass attractor. Well, I haven't gone that far yet, but any day now I fully expect to see an article in *BASSmaster* magazine on whether Tennessee sour mash is better than straight Kentucky bourbon!

I have attempted in the chapters that follow to classify lures according to the ways they can be fished or according to how they behave in the water. Although I think that such a classification will be useful to the reader, I certainly don't recommend that he always fish the lures only in the ways I have described.

In the discussions of the various types of lures, I have generally avoided color. It has been pretty firmly established that bass can distinguish between some colors, but they do not see colors the same way that we humans see them. I've caught bass on sky-blue lures, bright red lures, white lures, black lures, and so on. So far I haven't been able to make rhyme or reason of why a bass will hit a certain color at a particular time. But this does sometimes seem to be the case. Yet, I wonder.

Not long ago, my brother and I were shiner fishing in a spot where I knew bass to be. We fished several hours without a strike. Then, suddenly, we got action and caught eight bass in about twenty minutes. They quit biting just as suddenly. I can't explain this, but I do know that we didn't change the color of the shiners just before they started hitting. If we had lucked into such a feeding spree just after having tied on a pastel-pink

Pistol Pete, we would have probably concluded that we had found the color they wanted.

In any case, I am convinced that color is not as important as action. I'm also certain that a lot of the color on most lures is a waste of pigment. A frog-colored top-water lure with a yellow bottom looks really good to a fisherman while the lure is encased in plastic on a display board, but from under the water only the yellow belly would be seen. And it wouldn't be the same yellow. It would be in "shade" and would appear darker than it did in the well-lighted tackle shop.

More and more, I've started buying lures first for action and second for color. If I have a wide choice of colors to choose from—and many lures come in dozens of shades—I'll buy either black or something that resembles the shiny scales of shiners and shad. There are exceptions, but I generally use black (or dark) lures in murky water and shiny lures in clear water. I also tend to use black early and late in the day as well as at night, shiny when the sun is high and bright, black when I am fishing deep, and shiny when I am fishing shallow. But let me quickly add that my enormous tackle box contains not only black and white. I've got enough pretty colored lures in it to decorate a Christmas tree, and I use all of them.

It could well be that the deeper one fishes, the more important color becomes. I've recently read a technical bulletin called "Spectrum Fishing," written by Stan Lievense of Best Tackle. Here's part of what was said: "Light is a composite of the light spectrum colors. When light penetrates water, its colors filter out in varying degrees. The chart [Figure 47] illustrates approximately the greatest depth at which each color in the spectrum is visible to fish in a clear water lake."

The chart is based on clear water with the sun directly overhead. Under these conditions, red would not penetrate deeper than 15 feet. In murky water, or with the sun at an angle to the water, red would not penetrate even that far. Note that the chart has no white and black "colors." Mr. Lievense says: "White, black, and the metallic finishes should be explained. White is an excellent gatherer of light rays and shows light in a diffused manner. Black is the absence of color. When practically all light is gone, black is advisable for maximum contrast. The metallic nickel and silver finishes reflect light rays like a mirror. Gold and brass finishes reflect the yellow rays."

Mr. Lievense, a former fishery biologist, may be on the right track, and he gives the following example of how to apply spectrum fishing:

Let's say we're on a fishing trip and we want to select the best color lure for conditions. If it's before 8:00 AM (or after 6:00 PM), we can

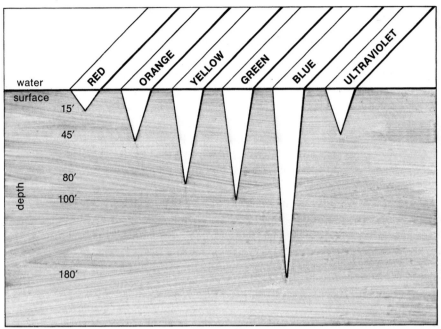

Figure 47

expect a very low light intensity, ruling out as a prime color the reds, oranges, and yellows. Our selection narrows to blue, green, white, or the nickel or silver finishes.

Now let's say the sun has risen above the 30 degree angle and we know we are getting better underwater lighting. Now we can start to consider the warm colors of red, orange, and yellow; yellow comes in as a good choice before orange or red. . . . Consider a dirty water lake in which one can see a lure only a few feet below the surface. The better penetrating blues and greens will likely be the best choices. Some turbidities filter out the blue end of the spectrum very rapidly, especially brown colored water. If this is the case, the yellow and brass finished lures are the most favored! Fishermen can determine this by eye. A yellow lure will show much sharper to the angler than a blue lure in brown stained water.

Anyone who wants to pursue spectrum fishing further should send 25 cents to Best Tackle for a copy of the bulletin. Personally, I find all this interesting, but I still put more stock in a lure's action and sonic vibration than in color.

Finally, let me say that the angler will miss a lot of fun by fishing a lure the same old way all the time. Vary the retrieve. Fish it slow. Fast. Fish it steadily. And erratically. Experiment.

Just this afternoon, for example, I made a little experiment that paid off. I went out to fish a few minutes, just to get away from the writing of this book. I tied on a Super Rooster Tail, a lure that I had never fished before. It's a sort of abbreviated safety-pin spinner bait; that is, the spinner doesn't ride very far back. This one was purple with a purple bucktail and a single hook (which I liked immediately). I anchored near a hole that I had just located a few days before, but I had not yet caught a single bass out of it. Maybe the bass hadn't seen a Super Rooster Tail, I figured. So, I anchored near the hole and cast out. According to the manufacturer the lure should be fished slowly, so I counted down and made a slow retrieve. The lure looked good to me, but I got no action in a dozen casts. The manufacturer also indicated that the lure could be jigged, so I jigged it for a dozen casts. Still not a bump. I decided that either no bass were in the hole or else they just didn't want that Super Rooster Tail.

I upped anchor and eased over to a patch of lily pads about 40 yards from the hole. Normally, I would have tied on a spoon, a plastic worm, or some such ultraweedless lure to fish out the pads. But the Super Rooster Tail was touted to be "extremely weedless and snag proof," and I rather doubted this claim because the hook was a good ways behind the safety-pin arm. Just for the hell of it, I put a 6-inch purple pork eel behind the lure and threw the combination into open water. It looked good, and I saw that it buzzed the surface nicely on a fast retrieve. (I have to admit that I like a fast retrieve and no doubt use it too often when a slower retrieve would be better.)

Holding the boat about 20 feet out of the pads, I cast the lure in. It hung up, but I decided to try it a few more times. On the third cast, a bass nailed it just at the edge of the pads. I worked the fish out into open water and soon boated it—a 7-pound beauty. But I discovered that I hadn't brought a fish stringer along. So, I pushed the bass under the pedestal seat and put my foot on him.

A few casts later, a real lunker grabbed the lure far back in the pads. For a while it was a deadlock. The bass just wallowed around. I knew I couldn't work it out of those thick pads, so I headed in to it, using the foot-controlled electric for all it was worth. It choked down. I took the paddle in one hand and held the rod in the other, but it is impossible to paddle a boat and keep a tight line at the same time. Also, my 7-pounder had got loose and was flopping all over the boat.

I decided to crank the kicker, but before I could do this the bass sounded and headed toward the boat, ducking a dozen lily pads under the water. Then the tugging on the line stopped, and the pads surfaced. The bass had either torn off or worked the hook loose.

The Super Rooster Tail was hung up, but I worked it free and started fishing again. The next strike came in open water, although I'm certain that the bass followed the lure out of the pads. It hit pretty close to me and kept coming, diving under the boat. After quickly loosening my star drag so that the fish could run, I maneuvered the boat with the electric until I was off the line. Then it was me and the bass in open water. We were fairly close to that deep hole now, and I'm certain that the bass was trying to get to it. The fish tried hard, but before long I had it in the boat. This one went a tad under 8½ pounds. By the way it pulled, though, I had thought it was larger.

Now I had two loose bass in the boat, so I decided to head for home. My wife didn't know what to say about the two bass. She had thought, no doubt, that I had been hard at work in my office inside the boathouse. She made some reference to the lawn, as if to say that if I had time to go out fishing, I had time to cut the grass.

"I wasn't *fishing*," I said. "I was out testing a lure!"

11
Fishing on Top

I HAVE HEARD SOME FISHERMEN SAY that they would rather catch one bass on top than five on bottom. I've said it myself. Some say ten. I've never gone that far, but a bass striking on top is surely one of the greatest of fishing thrills. I won't try to describe the action, but I will say that when a lunker strikes a surface lure there's no doubt about whether or not you're getting a bite!

The other night I was holding forth about top-water fishing to a staunch believer in the purple worm. He replied that he would rather catch one lunker on the bottom than no lunker at all. I couldn't help pointing out that the world's record largemouth—23 pounds and 4 ounces—hit on top and that a 17¼-pound bass was taken on a popping bug in West Lake Tohopekaliga. Further, I told him that the 10-pounder that took one of his purple worms away from him behind my house one Saturday was caught, worm and all, the following Monday morning on a Rapala twitching on the surface! He became so upset that I didn't have an opportunity to explain that it wasn't I who had taken the bass (*his* bass) on the Rapala. I never did correct his assumption. Somehow it made my point stick, barb and all.

Although I do enjoy fishing on top, the 10-to-1 comparison may be pretty

Top-water baits often prompt this kind of action!

close to the productivity ratio of underwater versus surface lures. If two anglers of equal ability were to fish in the same boat from dawn to dusk every day for a year, the one fishing the underwater lures would catch a good many more bass. But this isn't the whole story because the true bass-man does not fish a top-water plug when the bass are 35 feet deep.

In short, surface lures can be very effective at the right time and in the right place. The time is generally at sunset or sunrise. The place is usually some quiet, ripple-free spot where bass are feeding or bedding. I must point out, however, that I have caught 8-pound bass on surface lures at noonday—and in choppy water.

Dozens and dozens of lures are designed to be fished on top of the water. Many others are designed primarily to work under the surface but can be fished effectively on top. Still others can be fished on top for a few feet and then pulled under for the rest of the retrieve.

After studying the action of various surface lures, I attempted to classify them under appropriate headings. Some of the headings are rather arbitrary, and some lures could well fit into more than one category. Nevertheless, attempting to draw distinctions in their action helped me to see the differences between the various surface lures and to see the similarities in others. Anyhow, here's my breakdown:

Poppers. Designed to be fished slowly with a twitch/rest, twitch/rest motion, these plugs have a concave or scooped-out face, as shown in Figure 48. Such lures include Creek Chub's Plunker, Storm's Chug Bug, Cordell's Chopstick, and Heddon's Lucky 13.

As with most surface lures, the popper produces best very early and very late during the day. Fishing tactics of course vary from angler to angler, but I prefer to cast out and let the popper lie still until the ripples dissipate. Then I twitch it gently. Let it rest. Twitch it a little harder. Let it rest. Pop it. Let it rest. After three pops, I reel it in so that I can make another cast. Because I do reel the popper in often, I prefer one that has some sort of built-in action; the Lucky 13, for example, will dive and wiggle on a fast retrieve and will sometimes take a bass that might not have hit if the plug had been popped in slowly.

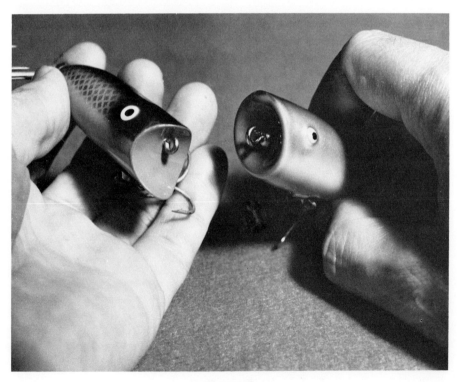

Figure 48

The theory behind my method of fishing the popper (and a lot of other surface lures) is that the plug looks like something that fell into the water. The fall dazed it, and it lies still for a while. Then it begins to recover, twitching a bit. After a few more twitches and pops, more lively now, it fully recovers and makes away fast. If a bass has been watching the thing and has any sense at all, it'll grab the lure before it gets away.

Darters. These lures—such as the Dalton Special and Creek Chub's Darter—differ from poppers in that they don't spray much water ahead because they don't have concave faces. They plunk and dart about instead of popping straight ahead. Some of these lures have a spinner on the tail, and others don't. I generally fish darters a little faster than poppers. I like to twitch them on first one side and then the other, making them zigzag in.

Gurglers. Designed with a built-in action, these lures are reeled straight in without imparting any action with the rod tip. Usually, the gurglers have some sort of curved metal plate up front that makes the whole plug wobble. The Arbogast Jitterbug, Figure 49, is the classic example. Most anglers

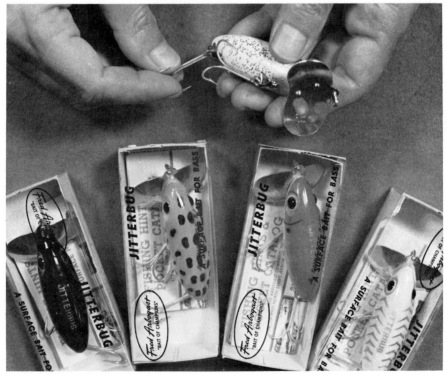

Figure 49

simply cast these lures out and reel them in. Even though this method will catch bass, it is sometimes better to stop them every foot or so.

The gurglers are very good for night fishing because the noise and the steady retrieve make it easier for a bass to home in on the lure. The steady *gurgle-gurgle-gurgle* also reassures the night fisherman that his lure is behaving properly.

Stick plugs. The Virginia Slims of plugs, these bass catchers twitch about enticingly on the surface. When at rest in the water, the stick lures sit at an angle, as shown in Figure 50. The angle varies somewhat from lure to lure, and to some degree with different weights of line. Some fishermen alter the angle by pinching a split shot onto the tail hook. The heavier the shot, the greater the angle.

Lures in this class include Smithwick's Devil's Horse, Cordell's Boy-Howdy, and Bomber's Stick. Some models have no spinner, others have a tail spinner, and others have spinners both fore and aft. In general the stick plugs should be worked pretty much like popping plugs and darters. But of course they are quieter, especially the ones without spinners. In my experience, stick lures are more productive in clear water on a calm day, when not much of a ruckus is required to attract a bass.

Propeller lures. These lures, usually with propeller-type spinners fore and aft, are shaped more or less like blimps. In other words, they are fatter than the stick plugs. They float flat on the surface, and the main attraction is the propeller action. Sure lures include Cisco Kid's Topper, Creek Chub's Injured Minnow, and South Bend's Nip-i-Diddee. One model, Rogers' Hawg Hunter, has oversized spinners to make more ruckus on the surface.

Although the propeller lures do not dip up and down like the stick plugs, they are old reliable bass catchers. I usually fish these slowly (twitch and rest, twitch and rest) for a few feet, then start a steady retrieve. In murky water or at night, many of the strikes will come on a steady retrieve, which, I believe, helps the bass home in. Another tactic that is at times very effective is to retrieve the lure steadily for a foot or so, then rest it for a few seconds.

Snorkeling lures. Originally intended to be worked under the water, the highly popular safety-pin spinner baits are also effective on the surface. Actually, the lure's jig-head body runs an inch or two under the surface, and the top-riding spinner blade (or blades) burble the surface. There are a couple of dozen models of safety-pin lures, and they will be discussed in more detail in the following chapters. Maybe they should be discussed at more length here because they are at times very productive when fished on top! If they are properly balanced (and some aren't), they are easy to fish in this manner. Merely cast them out and reel them in just

Figure 50

fast enough to keep the blade's burble visible. It's best to start the retrieve the instant the lure hits the water or a little before.

Sputterbuzzers. Some in-line spinner baits are designed to be pulled fast across the surface, either in open water or in pads and weeds. There's not much the angler can do to impart action except crank away. Still, these baits catch a lot of bass, and at times they'll produce for me when all else fails.

Lures designed for sputterbuzzing include the Harrison-Hoge Weed Wing, the Arbogast Sputterfuss, and the Tony Accetta Spin Dodger. Arbogast also makes a plug, the Sputterbug, that has a buzzer attachment up front, and Burke has a Sputter-Spin attachment that will work in front of top-water plugs and various spoons. This attachment and the sputterbuzzer baits are shown in Figure 51.

I'll have to admit that the Weed Wing is one of my favorite lures, and I suspect that I use it as a sort of therapy. When I need to work off some steam, I'll grab a Weed Wing and head for the lake. Fishing these things is hard work. The lure has to be reeled in fast (a reel with a 5-to-1 retrieve ratio is desirable) to keep it up. Some bass anglers shun fast lures because they believe that lunker bass seldom hit them. Their objection may be valid when lunker bass are holed up in deep water, but when they are roaming the flats and weed beds looking for something to eat, they'll hit a fast lure. And I mean hit it. I know this because I have caught several real lunkers while cranking in a Weed Wing as fast as I could.

The Weed Wing is a fun lure, and often a bass will hit at one three or four times on a single retrieve. When this happens, many anglers slow the lure down when they should be cranking it like mad. In other words, try to take it away from the bass. But the Weed Wing is not for anglers who have cardiac problems; I've had 7- and 8-pounders hit these things right at the boat.

I sometimes use a sputterbuzzer to locate bass in lakes that have large fields of grass and weeds. Once the bass are located, I may switch to a slower lure. With an electric motor set on high and a Weed Wing, I can test-fish a lot of water fast. In short, I can cast out a Weed Wing and have it back in before you can say Red-Eyed Hofschneider.

Not all sputterbuzzers have to be fished so fast. The Sputterfuss, for example, is a good deal easier to keep up. And I fish the Weed Wing faster than necessary. I usually put a 6- or 8-inch pork eel behind it, whereas a pork frog would make it ride higher. The manufacturer, in fact, recommends that it be fished with a pork frog.

Rattler lures. Some time ago, I received a Diamond Rattler lure at a meeting of outdoor writers in Tallahassee, Florida. To be honest, I thought

Figure 51

it was a joke. Shaped like a Tampa Nugget cigar, the thing was solid blue with inset diamond eyes. According to the instructions, it had a hollow cavity that contained small metal balls, which were said to rattle when the lure was retrieved. It did indeed rattle when I shook it, but I doubted at the time that it would call up any bass.

A few months later, I tied the thing on while I was fishing a canal in the middle of the day, telling my fishing partner that I was going to try a secret weapon. (We hadn't had a strike, and I had thrown everything else in my tackle box.) The lure cast nicely, and I put it within inches of a grass bank ahead of the boat, with the intention of working it down the grass and "rattling" a bass out of the thick cover. But on the first twitch an 8¼-pound bass grabbed it. I had never been more surprised in my life, and my fishing partner's smirk was gone. I thought I had indeed found a secret weapon, but upon removing the plug from the bass's mouth I found that the fish had cracked it.

Later on I filled in the crack with epoxy glue. It produced several more nice bass until a lunker cracked it again and made off with the tail hook. So, I retired the plug. I dug it out again though while shooting the photographs for this book. Splitting it open, I found that the cavity was rather large and the metal balls rather small, as shown in Figure 52.

Today there are a number of rattler-type surface lures on the market, but most of them fall into one or another of the categories in this chapter. Cordell's Boy-Howdy stick plug and Chopstick popper both rattle. Generally, a rattler lure should be fished slowly. But also try them fast, especially in muddy water.

Finland minnow lures. Designed primarily for running under the surface, the balsa Rapalas and similar plastic lures are very effective when twitched about on the surface. My usual method is to cast them out, let them sit still

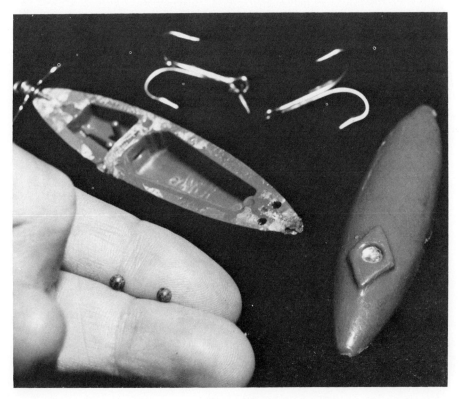

Figure 52

for a few seconds, then twitch-and-rest three times. If I don't get a strike by then, I reel them in at a moderate speed, making them dive under. Another effective technique is to retrieve the lure slowly and steadily, so that it wobbles along half under water and half on top.

The Rapala family is discussed more fully in Chapters 12 and 13.

Frog lures. There are several plastic and soft rubber frogs on the market. The better ones are designed so that their legs kick when the lure is jerked. With a little practice, one can coax these lures along so that they closely resemble the real thing. They'll catch fish, especially early and late in spring, summer, and early fall, when feeding bass are likely to keep an eye peeled for frogs.

Skittering lures. Some spoons, such as Eppinger's Dardevle, can be skittered across the surface on a fast retrieve, and Hildebrandt's Skitter-Spoon was designed for this method of fishing. Skittering will catch bass all right, but, personally, I prefer sputterbuzzing if I am going to use such a fast retrieve.

Snaking lures. When fished rather fast on the surface, some pork eels and plastic worms will swim like a snake. Although these lures will probably catch more bass if they are fished slower, snaking is a lot of fun when the bass are hitting on top. Once I took a nice string of bass, including a 7-pounder, out of Florida's Orange Lake by snaking pork eels late one afternoon.

12

Running Shallow

SHALLOW-RUNNING LURES are effective in early morning, in late afternoon, on cloudy or overcast days, at night, and during the spawning seasons. In short, shallow-running lures (or surface lures) should be used when the bass are in shallow water. This is obvious, but note well that a bass will not often rise from 20 feet down to hit a lure running a foot under the surface. The larger the bass, the less it is inclined to come up.

For my purposes in this chapter, I define shallow-running lures as any lure that, on a normal retrieve and without being allowed to sink before the retrieve is started, will run anywhere from 6 inches to 5 feet below the surface of the water. But the depth at which a lure runs is not easy to pin down, and it varies. The weight of one's line, the distance of the cast, and the speed of the retrieve all have a bearing on how deep some lures run. Note also that some lures can be classed as shallow or deep runners, depending on how one fishes them. Les Davis's Witch Doctor plug, for example, will run 20 feet deep when trolled with more than 100 feet of line out, but on a short cast it won't go down—at least not for me. I would classify it as a shallow runner, but anyone who trolled a lot would probably classify it as a deep runner. So, there is often room for argument.

Right or wrong, here's my breakdown:

115

Safety-pin spinner baits. Already mentioned in Chapter 11, these baits have a jig-head body, one or more top-riding spinners, and some sort of skirt, bucktail, or soft plastic body. Figure 53 shows a typical safety-pin bait.

The safety-pin design was invented some years ago, but the baits have become popular only during the past few years. Today everybody is making these lures: Cotton Cordell's Vibra Queen, Bomber's Bushwhacker, Rogers' Bass Rat, Zorro's Aggravator, Rebel's Destroyer, Shannon's Bass Bandit—to name only a few. Even some old-line baits, such as Mepps and Hawaiian Wiggler, are now available in safety-pin designs.

Figure 53

Because of the top-riding spinner arm, these lures are fairly weedless and can be fished effectively in grass and over brush. I normally use a pork rind on safety-pin lures, and I find that a 6-inch pork eel has a very good wiggle. Most of the safety-pin lures run about 3 feet deep on a normal retrieve. They can be reeled in steadily or bumped along the bottom.

A hot newcomer, the Little Jewel, was designed for fishing in very shallow water. Instead of a hunk of lead for the body, it has a spoonlike shape, which makes it ride higher. Thus it can be fished very shallow at very slow speeds.

In one brand or another, safety-pin lures are available in several sizes, all manner of colors, and with different size spinners. Some have interchangeable spinners. And spinner size can be important. The larger spinners (and I have one as big as a half dollar) produce more flash and louder sonic vibrations, and they should be fished in murky water; the smaller spinners, in clear water.

Some anglers prefer tandem spinners (one behind the other), some prefer twin spinners (one on either side), and some prefer a single spinner. I don't think it makes too much difference as long as the spinners spin and the bait is properly balanced. If my experience is any indication, the single spinners with good ball-bearing swivels are less likely to malfunction.

Front (in-line) spinners. The Hawaiian Wiggler (Figure 54), the larger Mepps baits, the Snagless Sally, the Panther Martin, as well as a dozen similar baits with front spinners, will all catch bass. Typical spinners run from 1 to 4 or 5 feet deep on a normal retrieve, but of course they can be fished deeper if you let them sink down before you start the retrieve. Most spinners have a skirt or bucktail, and I usually add on a pork rind or a 4-inch piece of plastic worm. Although I sometimes twitch these baits along, I believe that a steady retrieve is as good as any.

I am fond of making up my own spinner lures. A Peck's Silver Doctor streamer fly with a Hildebrandt's No. 4 gold Idaho spinner and a 4-inch Pedigo yellow lizard pork bait is one of my favorite lures for fishing in shallow water. Other combinations are almost infinite; a suitable spinner with a weighted Yellow Sally streamer and a 4-inch white bass strip pork rind, for example, is very effective at times.

I've never liked the Shyster-type spinners for most bass fishing because they are so small and have such little hooks. But this may be a personal prejudice. I know of one 10-pound largemouth that was taken on a small Shyster while the angler was fishing for crappie!

Tail spinners. The tail spinner is one small lure that I do like. Since the body is made of lead, they are quite heavy for their size and they cast beautifully even into strong wind. In addition to the small lead body, they

Figure 54

have a tail spinner and a single treble hook hanging from the belly, as shown in Figure 55. Examples include Mann's Little George, Bagley's Submarine Shad, Garcia's Dazzle Tail, Hildebrandt's Jigolo, and Lindy's Coach Dog. There must be a dozen others.

Tail spinners can be fished at various depths and at various speeds. They'll catch bass on a steady retrieve, and they can be hopped along by quick jerks. They can also be fished by long sweeps of the rod tip, but this method is usually more effective in deep water.

Anyone who fishes the tail spinners fast and shallow may want to take a tip from Tom Mann, who says that they should be retrieved as soon as they hit the water so that air bubbles will be trapped under the spinner. This will cause some sort of violent sonic reaction that may attract bass from some distance. The effect, however, will not last for more than the first foot or two of the retrieve. The best way to get this effect is to start cranking the reel handle and raising the rod tip fast as soon as the lure hits down. A long rod and a reel with a fast retrieve ratio help.

Finland minnows. At one time, the Rapala (Figure 56), a balsa lure made in Finland, was catching as many lunkers as plastic worms. After an article on the Rapala appeared in *Life* magazine, the lures were in great demand

Figure 55

and short supply; at the time, I heard that they were being sold for as much as $30! The Rapala craze has died down now, but the lures will catch as many bass as ever. As the illustration shows, they closely resemble shiners.

Since the Rapala came out, a number of plastic imitations have hit the market. They will all catch bass, but in my opinion the balsa Rapala is still the best—except that the damned things are very difficult to cast accurately. It is almost aerodynamic. So far as I know, the only other balsa lure of this type is Bagley's Bang-o-Lure. It will catch a lot of bass, but it doesn't cast any better than the Rapala.

The original Rapala had very light hooks, but some of the newer models (such as the Magnum Rapala) have larger hooks and are made of hard, heavier wood (African Odoum). They cast much better, but the action isn't the same. A small split ring will improve the action on most of the Rapala models, especially if heavy, stiff monofilament line is used. (The Bang-o-Lure comes with a split ring already attached.) Many anglers use a swivel snap instead of a split ring, but that's too much hardware up front to suit me. Besides, I've had bass straighten out those safety-pin-type snaps!

Figure 56

In lunker country, try fishing with 7-inch Rapalas. You'll miss some yearling bass, but the larger lure casts better than smaller ones and may interest a real trophy bass.

On a normal retrieve, a regular Rapala will run about a foot deep. Speeding up the retrieve won't make it run much deeper. A steady retrieve will catch a lot of bass, but I prefer to jerk mine along. One favorite method of fishing the Rapalas is to twitch them about on the surface, as was discussed in Chapter 11.

A sinking model, the Countdown Rapala, is discussed in Chapter 13, and couple of deep-diving Rapalas are discussed in Chapter 17.

Sonic vibrators. These heavy, shad-shaped lures have an eyelet on top and well back from the front. Whopper Stopper's Bayou Boogie, Cordell's Spot, Smithwick's Water Gator, and Bomber's Pinfish are shown in Figure 57. These lures typically have a fast, tight wiggle, which causes sonic vibrations that attract bass. Some of them also have a built-in rattler.

A good many anglers would classify these baits as deep runners, but I believe that most of them run from 3 to 5 feet deep at normal casting dis-

Figure 57

tances and on a relatively fast retrieve. You can fish them deeper by letting them sink down and reeling in slower, but these lures should normally be retrieved fast in order to get the full sonic effect.

These lures are relatively heavy for their size, and they cast nicely. They are very popular in some locations as trolling lures. When casting, I usually fish them with a steady retrieve, but I also jerk them along or fish them with a start/stop retrieve by first reeling very fast and then stopping for a second or two.

Swimming lures. These plugs, Figure 58, are characterized by a metal lip, which makes them dive under and wiggle on the retrieve. Some, such as the Cisco Kid's, have adjustable lips; by bending the lip up or down, one can adjust, to a degree, the depth at which the lure runs.

All these lures of good quality will catch bass and are old favorites with some anglers. Most people fish them simply by casting out and cranking in.

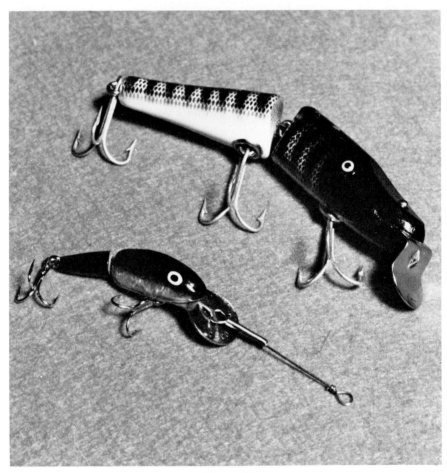

Figure 58

This method works because the lures have built-in action, but at times they are more effective if they are retrieved in jerks, imparting action with the rod tip. Incidentally, the world's record largemouth was caught on a swimming lure being twitched on the surface! The lure was Creek Chub's No. 2401 Wiggle Fish.

Another type of swimming lure has a built-in plastic lip. It is shad-shaped and runs shallow, which makes it especially effective at times when the bass are feeding shallow in large, shad-filled impoundments. These lures have good action, but some of them are light and as difficult to cast as the Rapala. Figure 59 shows Bomber's Speed Shad and Storm's ThinFin Silver Shad.

Figure 59

Alphabet plugs. At the time this chapter is being written, a hot new plug has suddenly become the thing. As described in the 1973 July–August issue of *BASSmaster* magazine, it "looks like a pregnant guppy, has better moves than a hopped-up go-go dancer, and costs even more than a prime-cut New York strip." The lures were originally carved by hand from balsa, but production was limited. The lures were in great demand at bass-fishing tournaments, and some were sold, or rented, at fancy prices.

But now there are several production models out, and some of them have a built-in rattler. So many lure makers are cashing in on the craze with so many nearly identical lures and such similar names that it's easy to confuse them. We already have Bagley's Big B, Cordell's Big O, Norman's Big N, Storm's Fats-O, Mann's Fat Albert, Rogers' Big Jim, and Heddon's Big Hedd, and others will no doubt be forthcoming. All these plugs are made of plastic, except the Bagley's balsa model. Figure 60 shows some production models, but so far I haven't been able to obtain one of the hand-carved plugs. My nephew made one for me out of balsa, however, and it has been quite productive.

Figure 60

The secret of the plug's success lies in its buoyancy and its wiggle, which apparently sets up an appealing vibration in the water. Bill Norman described his Big N as a "floating, diving, wobbler." He added that some fishermen prefer a very, very fast rate of retrieve, and others prefer a medium to fast retrieve. Some anglers twitch them about on the surface a few times, then retrieve steadily. Another effective tactic is to reel them in fast, then stop reeling for a second or two, imparting a diving/rising motion.

Spoons. There are all manner of spoons, and most of them will catch bass.

The Johnson spoon is one of my favorite baits. It is bullet-shaped and casts nicely. And it's quite weedless. I always fish spoons of this type with a pork rind, a skirt, or a soft plastic worm.

These spoons run at almost any depth, depending on the rate of retrieve, so that they can be fished in any situation. But in my experience they are most effective in shallow water, weeds, and lily pads. They can be jerked and twitched along, but most anglers simply reel them in at a modest rate of retrieve. The wobbling action of this type of spoon can be improved by using a split ring, especially when using small spoons with heavy monofilament line.

Recently I've had good luck with a ½-ounce black Johnson spoon trailed by a 9-inch black, supersoft Uncle Josh pork eel, as shown in Figure 61. The spoon and the eel make the bait almost a foot long, and I like to snake it slowly and steadily along the bottom in shallow water.

The Dardevle-type spoons, Figure 62, usually have a single treble hook, but Eppinger does make some Dardevles with weedless single hooks. These spoons are known fish getters, but their reputation was made primarily in northern waters on lake trout, muskie, and pike. They will no doubt take bass anywhere, but, personally, I've never cottoned to them.

The Dardevle can be retrieved at various depths, and you can easily change the depth by slowing down or speeding up the retrieve. The lures have a built-in wobble, so that a steady retrieve is sometimes effective. They can also be fished by darting them along, by skittering them across the surface, or by jigging them up and down in deep water. In shallow water, I've had better luck with these spoons by twitching them along gently. I never fish them at a fast retrieve (except when skittering) because they tend to cause line twist.

There are also a few swimming spoons that wiggle instead of wobble. Hildebrandt's Voo Doo, Figure 63, is a good one. With a short cast and a heavy line, it runs about 3 or 4 feet deep. Speeding up the retrieve will not make it dive deeper, but it will make it wiggle faster and more erratically. I usually fish this lure with a 4-inch pork rind behind it.

Figure 61

Figure 62

Figure 63

Buck Perry's Spoonplug is another spoon of the swimming type, but it is a deep runner and will be discussed in Chapters 13 and 17.

Plastic worms. These bass catchers were discussed at length in Part Two. Let me repeat here that in shallow water I prefer to fish the worm without a weight because I want it to sink slowly. Bass will often take the worm while it is going down, so watch the line very closely for a telltale twitch.

Boomerang-shaped lures. Helin's Flatfish, the Lazy Ike (Figure 64), and Heddon's Prowler are all shaped rather like a boomerang. They will all catch bass, and they have an enticing wiggle. These lures run at various depths, depending on the model, size, and weight, but for the most part they are shallow runners. Most of them will not dive deeper on a faster retrieve; they'll just wiggle more.

In addition to the boomerang lures, I'd like to mention an S-shaped lure (I don't know where else to categorize the thing). It's the Heddon Cousin, Figure 65. It runs rather shallow and resembles a snake or an eel. Although it actually wiggles from side to side, it gives the appearance of moving up and down!

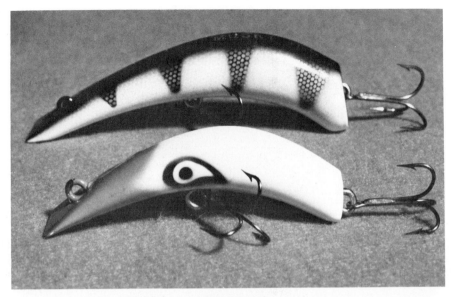

Figure 64

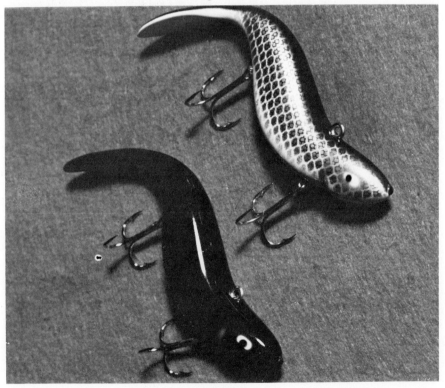

Figure 65

13

Going Deep

NOT MANY YEARS AGO, almost all bass were caught in relatively shallow water simply because that's where people fished for them. They plugged the bank and visible cover. Unless they fished early in the morning, late in the afternoon, at night, on cloudy days, or during the spawning season, they were unlikely to come in with full stringers. Today, any knowledgeable angler knows that bass are in deep water more often than not, and he'll have a number of lures suitable for, or in some cases designed for, fishing deep down.

Some top-water lures and shallow runners can be fished deep by weighting them down. If a heavy sinker is attached about 20 inches above the lure, it will of course run deeper during either casting or trolling. Such lures can be fished with a steady retrieve or by imparting action with the rod tip; however, the sinker will have an influence on the action finally imparted to the lure. I usually avoid this rig because I don't like the way it casts. Plug and lead whirl around like a planetary system, and sometimes they foul the line. But I have used the rig on occasion, and I will no doubt use it again from time to time.

Many of the spinners, spoons, and other shallow-running lures can be fished very deep by the countdown method. The trick here is to know how fast a lure sinks. Some lure makers publish this information, but most don't.

The sinking rate for any lure can be determined pretty accurately if the angler will take the trouble to find out how deep the water is under his boat and count the number of seconds it takes the lure to hit bottom. But a stopwatch isn't necessary. Counting down by thousands (1,000, 2,000, 3,000, etc.) is usually close enough. If a lure sinks 1 foot for each 1,000 count, and if you want to fish 17 feet deep, simply cast it out, count to 17,000, and start the retrieve.

Not many lures are designed to run very deep unless they are allowed to sink down. But a few big-lipped plugs will go down on a fast retrieve, and some heavy, compact lures, such as lead jigs, will go deep on a slow retrieve. Here's my breakdown on deep runners and some lures that are suitable for fishing with the countdown technique:

Deep Divers. A few years ago, I was fishing with my nephew in a 50-acre man-made lake in Mississippi. We called it Jungle Pond because the man who made it had flooded a thick creek bed, letting the trees and brush stand. There was a lot of deep water, and virtually the whole lake was "structure." We had been taking some bass by casting Rapalas and other plugs into pockets or around treetops and logs, but that day the bass weren't hitting, and I figured that they might be deeper.

I tied on a Hellbender, a floating diving plug. Seeing the big snout and knowing that the lure would dive into all that submerged brush, my nephew said, "You're not going to throw that thing out there, are you?"

I did just that.

"You'll never get it back," he said as the Hellbender hit the water.

I cranked it in. It ran into all manner of tree limbs and brush, but it either came right through or tripped over all the obstructions. Closer to the boat, however, it did get hung—into a bass!

After fishing these lures for a number of years, I am still amazed at how they get through, or over, tree limbs and brush. The reason lies in the design of the lure. It has a long snout—about half as long as the lure's body—and the eyelet is well back from the end. The lure comes through the water at an angle, snout down. When it roots into a limb, a log, or a rock, the line trips the lure over. The lure then straightens up and comes along its merry way. If it does hang up, it will often float free if the angler will give some slack to the line.

In addition to Whopper Stopper's Hellbender, there are a number of lures in this class, as shown in Figure 66. Some of these have eyes on the rear end and look like something swimming backward. The deep divers include Arbogast's Mud-Bug, the Bomber, Gudebrod's Bump 'n' Grind, Storm's Hot'n Tot, Cordell's Crab, and Rogers' Craw-Pap. And there must be a dozen others.

Most of these lures run from 5 feet deep on a slow-normal retrieve to 20

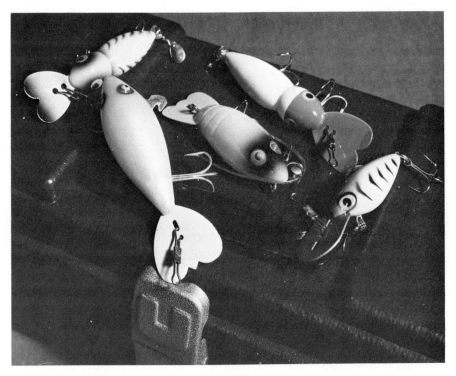

Figure 66

or 25 feet deep on a fast retrieve. The length of the cast and the weight of the line have a bearing on the depth attained.

All these lures have caught an awful lot of bass, especially on impoundments. They are effective in fishing some types of underwater structure, and they are ideal for fishing earth dams and inclined riprap. The trick is to anchor away from the dam, or move the boat parallel to it, and cast right up to the water's edge. Crank the bait in, adjusting the rate of retrieve so that the plug follows the slope of the dam, occasionally bumping into the dirt or the riprap. The same principle can be used on any fast slope, such as some riverbanks and points in some lakes.

By the way, these lures will stay deep longer than some other lures. Whereas a spoon or a jig will tend to come up as it gets closer to the boat, the Hellbender is always trying to dive deeper. In fact, these lures pull pretty well even without a fish on, and fishing them for long periods can become hard work. On a fast retrieve, they'll run under the boat while you're trying to get them in! Noting this tendency while we were fishing our Jungle Pond, my nephew asked me whether I needed the landing net to get the plug out of the water!

Deep swimmers. Most lipped swimming lures, such as the Pikie, run rather shallow, but a few are designed with very large lips and will go down from 8 to 20 feet. (The lips on these lures are set at an angle to the body instead of sticking straight out like the snouts on the Hellbender lures.) The Rapala Deep-Diver is a good example of this type of lure. It is fished pretty much like the Hellbenders, but it doesn't swim at as much of an angle and therefore doesn't trip over underwater obstructions as nicely. There are two sizes of these Rapalas, and each runs at a different depth. They are discussed more fully in connection with trolling in Chapter 17.

Cordell's Huncho, Figure 67, is another deep swimmer. It's a floating lure with a long plastic lip. It's a little hard to believe it, but it stays shallow on a fast retrieve and goes deeper on a slow retrieve!

Spoonplug. Here's another one of those weird-looking baits that bass anglers might have laughed at when they first appeared some years back. The Spoonplug runs deep, but the exact depth is related to the size and weight of the lure. The complete spoonplugger will have a whole set of

Figure 67

these baits. Although the Spoonplug can be cast, it is usually thought of as a trolling lure and will be discussed further in Chapter 17.

Countdown lures. Almost any sinking lure can be fished deep, and at fairly accurate depths, by the proper use of the countdown technique. Note, however, that most lures will tend to come up toward the surface as they approach the boat. The only way to keep them down at the desired depth is to reduce the rate of retrieve as the lure approaches the boat. To do this properly requires good timing—and some practice. In any case, here are some of the more appropriate lures for counting down:

Tail spinners are in my opinion ideal lures for counting down. For one thing, they sink fast. For another, the tail spinner works nicely while the lure is sinking. Thus, many of the strikes come before the angler starts fishing the lure! Holding a tight line after a long cast and following the lure down is the best policy with these lures. The slightest bump or twitch can mean that a large bass has engulfed the lure.

Front spinners can be counted down effectively. A slow retrieve is usually required to keep them down, but note that some of these baits tend to run deeper than others. The Hawaiian Wiggler, for example, comes in three models, all of which run at different depths for a given rate of retrieve. The 200 series runs shallow; the 150 series, medium; the 100 series, deep.

Safety-pin baits have some spinner action—some wobble and some flutter—but the spinners don't spin as nicely as could be desired while they are sinking down, although some models do work better than others in this respect. One upside-down safety-pin design, however, does have good spinner action on the fall. It's Rebel's Drop-Spin. It has a weight on the spinner arm, and both the spinner and the hook ride down on the retrieve or when the lure is falling.

Jigs fall fast, so that the countdown is short. They will catch bass either by jerking them along, by pumping them with long sweeps of the rod, or by merely reeling them straight. I prefer to use jig heads as a weighting device for pork and plastic attachments. One effective bait, which has been used for some time in salt water but which is fairly new in bass fishing, is a jig head with a soft plastic grub behind it. This bait is sometimes surprisingly effective on a steady retrieve without any rod-tip action. Most of the plastic-worm manufacturers market a grub of some sort, and many firms are now putting out grub-jig packages. Examples include Stembridge's Fuddlebug, Cordell's Grubby, and Rebel's Hot Tail.

Spoons of the wobbling kind usually run shallow on a normal retrieve. They can be fished deep by counting down and retrieving slowly. Some spoons have some flutter action while they are falling, and bass will sometimes take them while they are going down.

Sonic lures, such as the Spot, work very well with the countdown technique. They are at their best, however, on a fast retrieve, which will make them come up after the countdown. One technique that will produce plenty of vibration and rattle is to count the lure down and then retrieve in long, quick sweeps. Follow each sweep with a pause to let the lure fall back down.

Countdown Rapalas are made especially for the countdown technique. They cast much, much better than the balsa Rapalas, but the action isn't as good. They'll catch bass on a slow, steady retrieve at the countdown depth, but I think they are more effective if they are twitched along. A good many anglers may not agree, but I would rather use the regular balsa model behind a weight.

14

Bumping Bottom

MANY OF THE DEEP-RUNNING LURES and most of the countdown lures can be used to bump or root the bottom. Actually, it's a good deal easier—and is usually much more productive—to bump bottom than to fish at, say, 19 feet in deeper water. It's more effective because bass are usually on or near the bottom, and it's easier because the angler can tell when his lure touches down, whereas it's difficult to know when it is running 19 feet down in water that may be much deeper. The fact is that bottom bumping is usually the best way to fish for bass. The exceptions are when the bottom is covered with moss, silt, and so on (in which case it's better to count down and fish just off the bottom), and when bass are suspended at some depth under a school of shad, or suspended because of oxygen stratification.

When you use sinking lures for bottom bumping, the trick is to cast out and keep a tight line. When the line goes slack, the lure has touched down (unless a bass has taken it). Once on bottom, it can be snaked, hopped, or pumped along. When you are using deep divers to root the bottom, cast out and retrieve fast until you feel bottom, then slow down and adjust the retrieve to keep the lure touching down from time to time.

Of course, appropriate lures can be bumped or rooted along the bottom in either shallow water or deep. On most lures, however, the action will be different at various depths. Assume, for example, that a fast-sinking lure is cast 50 feet in very shallow water. When it is pumped with a long sweep of the rod, the lure will scoot along in almost a straight line near the bottom; when the same cast and the same retrieve are used in 20 feet of water, the lure will come farther off the bottom. So, the depth of the water has a bearing on how a bottom bumper, or a rooter, should be fished. The type of bottom is also an important consideration. When you are fishing in underwater grass, for example, a long upward sweep would be better than a short hop, and an ultraweedless lure would be better than one with treble hooks.

Jigs. Nylon or hair jigs are natural bottom bumpers, not only because of their shape and size, but also because they cast well and sink fast. Jig heads with pork or plastic attachments are quite effective for bass; in fact, Gapen's Hairy Worm is one of the most productive lures I've ever used.

If I'm fishing a jig off the bottom, I prefer to work it with short 6-inch hops, or (at times) use a steady retrieve. But when bumping bottom with jigs, I prefer to work the jig slower, with somewhat longer sweeps.

Jig-L-Worm. Designed especially for bottom bumping, Creek Chub's new Jig-L-Worm looks very good to me, and I've heard of some mighty large catches on it. The head sinks and the two jointed-tail sections float, so that when pulled or jerked along the bottom it resembles some eel-like creature feeding. It can also be jigged and jerked with rod-tip action, or by starting and stopping the retrieve. See Figure 68.

Worms and eels. These baits are the greatest of the bottom bumpers, especially when properly rigged and weighted. For a full discussion, see Part Two.

Spoons. The various kinds of wobbling spoons, especially the weedless ones, can be bumped and scooted along the bottom with either a jigging motion or a slow, steady retrieve. Cast the spoon out and let it sink—and be ready for a strike while the spoon is going down. If spoons are to be fished slowly on the bottom, they are more effective when used with a pork rind.

Spoonplugs. This bait is a good bottom rooter, especially in sand. Cast it out, let it sink down, and retrieve it steadily and rather fast.

Deep divers. As I pointed out in the last chapter, these lures can be rooted along banks and inclines. They can also be rooted along flatter bottoms provided that they run deep enough. They work well over hard bottoms, especially rock, but not in mud or silty areas.

Tail spinners. These lures are effective for touching bottom in connection with pumping techniques. One big reason for their effectiveness is that the spinner works while the lure is coming up and while it falls back down.

Many of the strikes will come on the fall. They'll often hang up on some bottoms, but the single treble hook is light and can usually be pulled free with a strong line.

Safety-pin spinners. Most of the safety-pin lures can be bumped along the bottom successfully. I prefer to reel mine along with a slow, steady retrieve, letting them touch down from time to time. Some anglers pump them in, but I prefer a tail spinner for this technique, except that the safety-pins are more snag-proof.

Floating plugs. Some floating plugs, such as the Finland minnow, can be fished on or very near bottom by adding a heavy sinker about 20 inches up the line from the lure. The sinker can be pulled or bumped along the bottom

Figure 68

slowly, and the lure will float up slightly off the bottom. The exact action will depend on the kind of plug used, the kind of sinker and its weight, and the distance between the sinker and the plug. One tactic to try is to jerk the rig along with an occasional pause. Or let the lure sit suspended in the water and occasionally twitch it, just as you would a surface lure. But it's best to experiment with this sort of rig in clear water (a swimming pool is ideal) before trying it on a serious fishing trip.

15

Fishing
Underwater Structure

AN EXPERT BAIT CASTER, who can put a plug into a tiny pocket in surface grass and lily pads, or within inches of the shady side of a stump, will sometimes catch a lot of bass. But not always. The expert bottom bumper will sometimes catch a lot of bass, but at times it will be possible to bump the bottom all the way across a lake without a bass even seeing the lure. Anyone who can count down and run a lure at a precise depth can sometimes mop up on schooling bass and larger bass suspended under the school, but most often fishing a lure at, say, 15 feet in open water is a waste of time.

By far the most consistent bass angler is the one who knows how to fish "structure." Structure is a fairly new term in the literature of angling. Broadly, it means any irregularity on the bottom of the lake that "holds" bass. In other words, it is a place where bass hang out. Usually, it will provide cover and shade. Most often it will be in, or near, deep water. Structure, then, might be a treetop, a ledge, rocks, and so forth. Most natural lakes do not have as much structure as impoundments, so that visible cover, such as weed beds and lily pads, gains in importance as bass hangouts. Large impoundments, on the other hand, usually have a wide variety of structure: submerged islands, creek banks, brush, standing timber, roadbeds, ditches, old bridges—even buildings and excavated graveyards.

Further, the bassman must in many cases locate substructure. This is an irregularity in the structure. Examples of substructure include a bend in a creek bed, a sharp curve in a submerged road, intersecting fencerows in a submerged field, and so on.

The modern bass angler's success often depends on how well he can locate structure and substructure. Although it is possible to find holding structure by trial and error, by systematic sounding, or even by scuba diving, the best bet is to use a good depth finder and a topographic map. The map, based on photographs of the area before it was flooded, gives the angler a general guide to what the bottom looks like, and the depth finder helps him pinpoint particular spots.

How structure should be fished depends on a number of factors, such as what sort of structure it is, how deep it is, what sort of tackle the angler has, and so on. I might add that some bass anglers will never learn how to fish

This photograph was taken while the Amistad impoundment was filling on the Texas–Mexico border. The house is now under water. Such structure often provides excellent holding spots for bass. In this case, a lure fished yo-yo fashion around the veranda might pay off.

submerged structure because they don't stay with it. They like to plug a bank, they have always plugged a bank, and they always will—even when the bass are in 20 feet of water in the middle of the lake. Few of these anglers are too narrow-minded to try new methods, but their first attempts at structure fishing are not too successful, and they don't stay with it long enough.

I like to cast a bank and visible cover too—it's my favorite kind of fishing—but I also like to catch bass, and I am certain that 90 percent of one's fishing time should be spent in working submerged structure and bottom irregularities and 10 percent in fishing visible cover. Fishing structure requires not only more skill but also more knowledge of bass and their habits. It requires knowledge of where bass are likely to be at a particular time of the day in a certain season of the year. Will they be holding somewhere, or will they be heading for feeding grounds along a migration route? It requires skill in reading a depth finder and forming an image of the bottom. It requires skill in counting down a lure, and knowledge of how lures behave while sinking or while bumping into structure. One has to learn to distinguish instantly between a bass strike (or bump) and a snag on a limb in a submerged treetop. In short, one has to attune one's senses to how a lure *feels* to an extent undreamed of by a plugger of the old school.

Some structure, such as a submerged roadbed, can be fished by bumping or rooting bottom, as discussed in the last chapter. Other techniques include:

Yo-yoing. Sometimes called doodlesocking and a number of other names, yo-yoing is a technique for fishing structure directly under the boat. The lure is lowered to the structure and jiggled up and down. The method works best in deep water, but it can be used at 20-foot depths in murky water. The more shallow and clearer the water, the quieter the fisherman must be.

Yo-yoing is the ideal technique for fishing in submerged timber. Sometimes it is the only method of fishing timber successfully, especially when the treetops are submerged. If, for example, one casts out into submerged timber, the lure would be likely to hang up before it got anywhere near the bottom; if the lure is dropped straight down, it is less likely to hit a snag.

Usually, a heavy lure is used for yo-yoing. Tail spinners, Texas-rigged plastic worms with heavy slip sinkers, jigs, and spoons are the favorite lures for yo-yoing. Some bassmen use long, thin spoons, which were designed primarily for saltwater fishing. Surprisingly, many of the more popular yo-yoing lures are not weedless!

Obviously, yo-yoing in very heavy structure requires a stiff rod and a heavy line (25- to 30-pound) so that an angler can horse a bass out or pull his lure free when it snags. A lure bumper also comes in handy. But the experienced yo-yoer will not lose as many lures as a top-water bait caster might think. The trick here is to learn to distinguish between a bass bump and a limb. If it's a bass, strike back hard. If it's a limb, give slack line and chances are that the lure will fall off. Developing and attuning this sense of touch is important so that you won't set the hook into a limb or give a bass slack line!

Many anglers use a bait-casting rig for yo-yoing, but a spinning outfit works better for me. With a bait-casting rig, one has to strip off line to get the lure down quickly. With spinning gear, the lure falls down almost freely if the pickup mechanism is disengaged. A push-button spincast reel works well enough, but an open-faced underslung reel is ideal in my opinion.

If you want to yo-yo at a specific depth, it is best to put an adjustable marker on your line so that you'll know how much to let out. A knotted rubber band (with the ends trimmed closely) or some sort of bobber stopper will work on bait-casting and spincast reels. The marker can be reeled onto the spool when the lure is pulled in; when you let the lure down again, pay out line until it reaches the marker.

With open-faced spinning reels, a rubber band of suitable size can be put on the spool, as shown in Figure 69. When the angler reels the lure in, hopefully with a bass on, the line winds on over the rubber band. When he lowers the lure again, the line will stop unwinding when it uncoils down to the rubber band. Note that the rubber band has to be inserted around the line, which means that it must be put on the reel before the line is run through the rod guides. This is simple with reels that have removable spools. Just let the lure fall to whatever depth it is to be fished, snap out the spool, put the rubber band around it from the rear, and snap it back in place.

Anyone who does a lot of yo-yoing will need a foot-controlled electric motor and a depth finder. Both of these are almost essential to hold a position directly over substructure. In fact, some bassmen are now mounting auxiliary transducer units on the bow, often on the shaft of the electric motor. If the stern-mounted transducer were used for yo-yoing, the man in the front seat would be reading the structure behind him instead of directly underneath.

Yo-yoing need not be restricted to heavy timber and similar structure. It can be used to fish on any bottom or to pinpoint a lure more accurately in a given structure. For example, you are fishing a large impoundment and have located a submerged rocky cliff that drops straight down. Bass—especially spotted bass—often lie against a cliff or around out-jutting layers of rock in such lakes as Lewis Smith in Alabama. Yo-yoing is a good way to present a lure in such a case.

Some anglers yo-yo by reeling the lure up and letting it back down by

Figure 69

releasing line. But most yo-yoers do not turn the reel handle until the lure is pulled in. Instead, they work the lure up and down by pumping the rod. Of course, the rod can be worked all around the bow and along the side of the boat.

Pass fishing. One way to fish such structure as underwater brush is to cast the lure beyond it and make a pass at it. Deep divers, such as the Hellbender, are very good for working structure in this manner, provided that the structure isn't too deep. The Hellbenders will come right through treetops, tripping over the limbs. Safety-pin lures, spoons, plastic worms, and pork eels can also be used effectively.

Nonweedless lures can be used to work underwater brush. The trick here is to work the lure on either side of the structure and on top of it. (Bass often lie suspended just on top of structure or to one side of it.) To do this, one must have the countdown technique down pat and must know exactly where the structure is in relation to the boat. When you are fishing particular structure with this method, it is best to locate the structure with a depth finder, then drop a marker off to one side of it. Next, move the boat to the other side and anchor it. Use two anchors so that the boat stays put. In this way, the marker makes a convenient reference point for casting.

To pass-fish successfully, one must get the lure close to the structure, which means that some lures will snag from time to time. This is to be expected and is even desirable; brushing a limb occasionally reassures the bassman that his lure is getting close enough to attract bass.

Fishing inclines and drop-offs. As already mentioned, a steep incline can be fished by yo-yoing. Another method is to pull a sinking or deep-diving lure down the incline if it isn't too steep. Still another method is to pull a suitable lure into (and up) the incline by casting from shallow water into deep. A good deal depends, of course, on how steep the incline is, so that methods, rates of retrieve, and so on will vary considerably.

With moderate inclines, say up to 45 degrees, bouncing or rooting a lure along the bottom while fishing downhill is effective. Deep divers fished in this manner (along dam riprap) were discussed in Chapter 13. Plastic worms, weedless spoons, tail spinners, safety-pin baits, and other sinking lures can be used effectively. You can also bump bottom while pulling the lure uphill. It's best to anchor or otherwise hold the boat near the top of the incline; if the boat is too far away from the top of the incline, the line would dogleg over the top and might cause you to lose a lunker bass.

Still another method, applicable to steep drop-offs, is to fish parallel to a line of previously dropped markers. The best procedure is to drop the markers on the shallow side of the underwater incline, then hold the boat at the edge of the incline and cast parallel to the marker line. Either use a deep diver or count a sinking lure down to the desired depth (or let it fall to the bottom). The closer the lure runs to the incline, the better are your chances of getting a bass.

It is best to drop markers along the shallow side of an incline if you want to move the boat along without anchoring it. For fishing downhill, keep the boat out in deeper water and move it parallel to the line of markers. Cast toward the markers in much the same way as you would plug the shoreline of a lake. For fishing uphill, work the boat along the line of markers and cast out into deep water. When using either method, stop the boat as soon as you catch a bass. Fish that particular spot thoroughly—where there's one bass, there's likely to be more.

16

Fishing in Weeds and Lily Pads

AFTER THE HUBBUB AND THE BABBLE of a national political convention in Miami, one of the state delegates stopped by my place to relax for a day or two. Since he was an old poker buddy of mine, he couldn't understand what I was doing here on Timucuan Island in Central Florida's Lake Weir, where, he said, nothing had happened since Ma Barker and her boys shot it out with the cops some years ago. But it sounded to him like a nice place to rest his feet and clear his mind, and I think he had visions of enjoying red sunsets and silent white egrets while keeping one eye on a red-and-white panfish bobber.

When he and his wife arrived at 6 P.M., he found the lake to be pretty much what he had expected, but he was surprised to learn that I didn't have a batch of crickets and worms on hand. Nor did I have a cane pole on the premises. It was too late in the day to rig up to fish the way he had envisioned, so we loaded a fly rod and casting outfit into the boat and headed for the shady side of the lake.

For the first few minutes, I eased the boat along a thick weed bank with the aid of the foot-controlled electric motor. After I had caught half a dozen bluegills on the fly rod while instructing my friend in its use, I turned it over to him. Before long he was catching bream right and left (even on his back cast), so I tied a ½-ounce Weed Wing onto the bait-casting outfit. Then I hooked an 8-inch white pork eel behind the Weed Wing.

After casting about 20 feet into the thick grass, I made a fast retrieve—as fast as I could crank the reel handle. The lure barely touched water, coming through the grass like a squirrel through treetops. Just as it hit open water and started gurgling steadily along, I noticed a swirl behind it. Something had spooked the bass, so I eased the boat out a little farther from the grass. On the fourth cast, a 2-pound largemouth nailed the Weed Wing just as it straightened out in open water.

"By George," my friend said, democratically, "I thought for a while that you didn't know how to cast, but you are actually fishing in that stuff!"

He inspected the Weed Wing and pork eel while I put the bass onto a stringer. "Why do you retrieve it so fast?" he asked.

I explained that I had to work the lure fast in order to keep it up and gurgling on top. The tactic behind my extremely fast retrieve was to draw the bass out of the hay and into open water.

But the biggest bass we caught took the Weed Wing back in the hay. The strike came so quickly that I believe the bass was rising as the Weed Wing came down. I set the hook almost as quickly, and the lunker came on out of the water, shaking its head violently. Then it splashed down and sloshed about in the grass like a hog. Keeping a tight line, I headed the boat into the grass with the electric motor and asked my political friend to help out with the paddle. Quickly we got back to the bass, and I fought it out with the fish at close quarters.

"You need a net," my friend said just as I reached down to put a bowling-ball grip on the bass's lower lip.

We didn't have any scales in the boat or at the house, but I knew we had a nice bass. My friend wanted some fish to take home "to impress the boys," he said, so I gutted the lunker and left the impressive head on it. My friend swears that the bass weighed 12 pounds back at his home in Alabama!

Anyhow, we came in about dark with one stringer holding thirty some-odd bluegills and the other holding ten nice bass, including the lunker and a 5-pounder. Incidentally, I changed lure colors at sundown, and the larger bass went for a black Weed Wing with a black pork eel.

After our fish fry that night, I suggested that we drive into town early the next morning for cane poles and worms. Maybe we could smell out a shellcracker bed. By George, he said, if it was just the same with me, he'd just as soon sling a Weed Wing if I had another one.

I did. The lure is one of my favorites, especially for fishing in grass and lily pads. But at times other weedless lures will catch more bass. When you are choosing a lure, consider how thick the growth is, what kind of growth it is, how deep the water is, and what the bass are doing there. If the bass have run into the hay on a feeding spree, they'll hit fast-moving surface lures, especially in warm water. If they are in the pads or grass for cover and shade, they'll hit better if lures are allowed to sink down in potholes.

I have fished in grass so thick that a Weed Wing would not go down. Although I've had 8-pounders hit at a lure in the treetops, it is best to switch to a ¾- or 1-ounce weedless spoon, preferably a bullet-shaped one such as the Johnson Silver Minnow. A lure of this weight and shape will hit water in places so thick that a lighter lure will not even get wet.

Choice of lure isn't the only consideration. Heavy tackle—a stiff rod and a strong line—helps in this kind of fishing. First, it's needed to handle large bass in thick growth. Second, no lure is completely weedless, and heavy tackle is needed to pull a lure free when it snags. There's nothing that slows down a fishing trip more than some sport using ultralight spinning gear with a 4-pound line in thick grass; he spends half his time going to his lure to avoid breaking it off.

Another effective technique for fishing potholes in grass, lily pads, or water hyacinths is jiggle fishing. A long, stout cane pole is used with a few feet of line on the end. Pork rind, plastic worms, jigs, and other lures are jiggled up and down in any opening in the vegetation. Jiggling will catch a lot of bass at times, but I've never cared much for it. If my limited experience is an indication, the jiggler will land more bass with a single-hook, nonweedless lure. Lures with small treble hooks should be avoided. Also, the successful jiggler will either wade or proceed very, very quietly in a boat.

Whether casting or jiggling, I prefer a light boat with a heavy-duty foot-controlled electric motor equipped with a weed guard. This helps get back in to the lunkers when they can't be worked out. Some of the larger bass boats are not, in my opinion, ideal for fishing thick weeds in shallow water. They are too heavy, and fishing from some of those deck-mounted pedestal seats is about like sitting on top of a stepladder. It's the profile that I object to. When the water isn't too deep, you can usually catch more bass from weed beds by wading than by fishing from a boat. It's easier to wade to a snagged lure than to plough a boat through the grass, and lighter tackle can be used effectively by the angler who is willing to get his feet wet. Although I sometimes use spinning gear and fly rods, I still think that a hefty bait-casting rig is the best bet for wrestling with lunkers in the hay.

The bait caster has a wide selection of lures suitable for fishing in grass and pads. Here's my breakdown:

Plastic worms. These are very good and very weedless. They will catch bass when snaked through the weeds, but they are usually more effective when fished slowly. Let them sink down in potholes. Let them rest on lily pads, maybe with a tail dangling off. If they climb the grass, let them dangle around out of the water. When you get a bite, set the hook immediately lest the bass hemstitch the line hopelessly. I usually avoid slip sinkers and jig heads when fishing in weeds and pads.

Pork lures. These excellent baits are often fished on spoons and other weedless lures, but they can be worked quite effectively alone on weedless hooks, unless they present casting problems. They are especially good in lily pads. Work them slowly. A wire-guard weedless "worm" hook works nicely, but I prefer smaller hooks than are normally used on (or in) plastic worms.

Safety-pin spinner baits. In thick grass, the spinner on these baits will flop about but won't turn properly all the time. I therefore prefer to cast them 10 or 15 feet into the grass and pull them out into a stretch of open water, hoping to draw a bass out. Any of the safety-pin baits will catch bass in thick weeds, but I prefer a slightly different design. The lures have a separate weed guard made of strands of stiff monofilament nylon, such as the Whopper Stopper Whirlybird (Figure 70).

Figure 70

Front spinners. In thin weeds and lily pads, the in-line front spinners, such as the Tony Accetta Spin Dodger, work very well either on top of the water or down under. Personally, I prefer to sputter them across the surface, except in cold or deep water. As pointed out in Chapter 12, some of these lures, such as the Weed Wing and the Hawaiian Wiggler Sputter-fuss, were designed to be fished fast on top. When you are fishing in-line spinner baits in weeds or pads where silt tends to clog the spinner, leave about an inch of monofilament sticking out from the knot. The dangling line causes the strands of silt to slide over the spinner.

Spoons. All types of weedless spoons are used for fishing weeds and lily pads. I usually fish these with an 8- or 9-inch pork eel, but I suspect that I would connect with a larger percentage of my strikes if I used a shorter eel. I'm always trying to interest a lunker, though, and I feel that a 14-pounder won't have any trouble taking the long bait. I usually fish a spoon slowly when I have attached one of those long eels. If I want to fish a spoon fast, skitter fashion, I'll usually put on a pork frog, which is shorter and wider than an eel.

Frogs and things. Plastic and rubber frogs (Figure 71) are at times very

Figure 71

effective in lily pads and in thin weeds, but they are too light to go down in thick stuff. I fish them with a start/stop motion, imparting the action by twitching the rod tip slightly. Sometimes I'll let the lure rest for half a minute.

Generally, frogs are more effective when bass are actively feeding in the weeds and lily pads, and they are less effective when the bass are merely lazing in the shade. They are also more effective very early and very late in the day.

Hair frogs and cork popping bugs, along with artificial mice and other creatures, can be fished in weeds, but these lures are handled better with fly rods or light spinning tackle. I use them from time to time, but I usually cast them to the edge of the grass instead of far back into it. This method can be effective along very thick grass banks, especially on the shady side.

The Dirtybird. I'm left with one lure that doesn't fit neatly into the categories discussed previously. It's Whopper Stopper's Dirtybird, Figure 72. This thing resembles a safety-pin lure without the spinner arm and with a large, upside-down lip on front. The upturned lip causes the lure to ride

Figure 72

high, and it can be skittered or wobbled slowly. I like it for fishing in
grass because it's heavy and casts nicely. When skittering it, I use a 4-inch
pork strip; when fishing it under the surface, I use a 6-inch pork eel.

Quite frankly, I don't think that choice of lure is as important when the
bass are feeding in weeds and pads as when they are out in deep water.
Out in the lake, the bass would normally be feeding on shiners and shad
or, over rocky bottoms, on slow-moving crayfish. But in weeds and pads
bass are on the lookout for minnows, frogs, snakes, small birds, muskrats,
and just about anything else that swims in the water or moves through
the grass. In short, matching the hatch is no problem when bass are feeding in weed beds. They'll hit anything. By comparison, I've seen schooling
bass in the middle of the lake that wouldn't touch anything I had in my
tackle box.

Merely fishing in grass, however, is no guarantee that you will fill a
stringer with bass. At worst, it can be a pain in the neck and almost a complete waste of time. It's a pain when you're using light tackle and lures
that hang up frequently in very thick grass. It's a waste of time when bass
aren't in the grass (although a few small largemouth usually are).

At best, fishing in thick stuff can be, in my opinion, the most exciting
form of bass fishing. It is of course nice to feel a bass bump a plastic worm
30 feet down, and it is exciting to see, hear, and feel a bass hit a Lucky
13 on top. But nothing in bass angling quite compares to watching a
shallow-running Hawaiian Wiggler in a weed bed and seeing a lunker part-
ing stems several yards from the lure and homing in fast! Often a bass
will hit a fast-moving lure five or six times, and right at the boat. I have
to admit that I never know quite what to do when a bass starts hitting
and missing, but I'm certain that it's a mistake to slow the lure down. Keep
it coming.

Just the other day, my brother-in-law and I were drifting through a large
field of thin grass on Lake Weir. I was casting a silver Weed Wing off
one side of the boat, and he was working the other side with a black one.
We had caught a few yearling bass when, suddenly, just after I had made
a long cast, I heard a splashing ruckus to starboard, almost as if my
brother-in-law had fallen into the water.

I whirled around to see what was going on, and he was halfway out
of the swivel seat peering at the swirling water. Then he sat back and
held up a naked rod. Even the line had fallen down through the rod
guides. The fish had hit and broken the line within a foot of the rod tip!

"What was it?" I asked.

"I don't know," he said, fiddling with the latch on his tackle box. He was nervous and had lost some color. I must have laughed. "Hell, man," he said, "I had already quit fishing and was watching you." He got the box open and spread out the trays. "I don't think I've got another Weed Wing. Have you got anything black that sputters?"

"I'll get yours back," I said, casting my silver Weed Wing to his side of the boat. I reeled it in fast, and something long and big hit it about 5 feet from the boat. It was a chain pickerel about as long as the boat was wide, but I didn't hook it. I would, however, have given $50 to have landed the thing and found my brother-in-law's black Weed Wing in its mouth!

So . . . my advice to anyone who fishes in thick weeds and lily pads is to get a stout rod, use a strong line, tie on a good sharp weedless lure, keep a firm grip on the rod handle—and don't quit fishing until the lure is safe in the boat!

17

Trolling

I SELDOM TROLL FOR BASS unless I'm fishing with kids or some novice angler who doesn't know how to cast. A few years back, trolling was a good way to locate bass in a lake, but modern depth finders and other gear permit the angler to pinpoint likely bass haunts more effectively than by trolling. If an angler has modern equipment and knows how to use it, or already knows a lake well, trolling is more or less a waste of time.

On the other hand, a lot of people enjoy trolling—I enjoy it myself—and pick up quite a few bass. A few experts, such as Buck Perry, the Spoonplug man, have caught an awful lot of bass by trolling. Usually, however, the expert will stop trolling and start casting whenever he catches a bass because there are likely to be others nearby. Why troll away from them? Why not stop and fish out that spot thoroughly?

A few competent fishermen do prefer trolling to casting, and some who have depth finders use them to find and map out a trolling pattern. Not long ago I was talking to a fishing camp operator at Cross Creek, Florida (Cross Creek connects Orange Lake to Lake Lochloosa in Central Florida). He said that the most consistently successful angler who fished out of his camp always trolled. He caught more and larger bass, usually. His method

154

was to map out a pattern with a depth finder and buoy markers. Then he trolled Spoonplugs and Hellbender-type lures up and down his course.

In any case, there is no doubt that the knowledgeable troller can consistently take more bass than the guy who rides across the lake dragging a plug behind the boat without any idea of how deep the water is and without much awareness of, or interest in, how deep his lure is running.

The first thing that a troller should decide is how deep the bass are likely to be whenever and wherever he is fishing. The second question is how to get a suitable lure to run at that depth. Some lures run deeper at higher trolling speeds, whereas others tend to come up. Within a given speed range, some plugs maintain the same depth but wiggle more, or wiggle less. With a large number of lures, the fisherman can have some control of depth by adjusting the speed of his boat. But there are limits.

Another control method is to adjust the length of the line that is out. The more line, the greater the depth at which some lures run, but there are limits to this method of control too. Letting out too much line will have little effect on the depth of the lure because the drag of the line in the water will cancel out the lure's built-in tendency to sink or dive deeper.

Many of the lures discussed in Chapter 12 can be used for trolling shallow, and many of the lures discussed in Chapter 13 can be used to troll deep. There is little point in discussing all these lures again, and the breakdown below includes only those lures that are, in my opinion, especially good for trolling. The breakdown also includes some trolling aids.

Spoonplugs. Shown in Figure 73, the Spoonplug was designed primarily for sounding out a new lake or impoundment by trolling. Actually, there is a whole family of Spoonplugs. Each model is designed to run at a certain depth, no matter how fast it is trolled. The lures are more effective if they are fished right on the bottom, rooting in occasionally and kicking up sand. (They don't work too well over mud or weed bottoms.) Part of the Spoonplug philosophy is that the lure helps the fisherman "read the bottom." The lures can be trolled fast, which permits the troller to sound out a lot of lake quickly.

Unfortunately, most tackle shops carry only one or two sizes of Spoonplugs, whereas the complete troller needs several sizes. The manufacturer (Buck's Baits) markets a five-pack of Spoonplugs, available in a variety of colors and finishes. The company also provides, or sells, a couple of helpful booklets and even publishes a newsletter.

If I trolled a lot, I'd certainly keep a couple of five-packs in my tackle box. But there are models not included in the basic five-pack, and some

Figure 73

are not "standard" Spoonplugs. Anyhow, here's a table of standard models and their running depths:

SERIES	WEIGHT (OUNCES)	DEPTH (FEET)
500	1/8	2–4
400	1/4	4–6
250	1/2	6–9
200	5/8	9–12
100	5/8	12–15
900	7/8	20
800	1	25

It may well be that Elwood "Buck" Perry, a onetime physics teacher from North Carolina, is the father of modern bass fishing. It was he who publicized the fact that bass are primarily bottom fish and spend most of their time in deep water. Even today in the age of electronic fishing, Buck's Spoonplug is a big fish-finding aid to anglers who don't have depth finders, light meters, and so on.

Other deep runners. Lures with big lips and snouts, such as the Hell-bender, are popular for trolling because they run deep and trip nicely over underwater brush. For trolling at random, these deep swimmers will catch more bass than shallow-running lures. (But there are exceptions of course.) The trouble with these lures is that it's difficult to know exactly how deep they are going. No one, to my knowledge, has worked out a Spoonplug-type system for these lures. Even though an awful lot of bass have been caught by trolling these lures, the angler must proceed pretty much on a trial-and-error, hit-or-miss basis until he learns from experience —if he learns at all—exactly what the plugs are doing at a certain speed with a given amount of line out.

The Rapala people, however, have worked out a limited system with their Deep Diver plugs. These are made of hardwood instead of balsa, and they have big metal lips. There are two models, both shown in Figure 74. The DD7 runs from 8 to 12 feet deep; the DD9, from 12 to 15 feet. (I hope they will add more lures to this line and work out a system with more range.) These lures can be trolled at high speeds and still maintain, or stay within, their respective running-depth range. I haven't trolled the Rapala Deep Divers with the motor wide open, but I've revved up so fast that the rod was hard to hold!

Figure 74

Sonic lures. Sonic vibrations—made with lures that rattle, have large spinners, or produce a tight, fast wiggle—will carry for long distances in the water and are five times faster than sound waves in the air. Lures that create sonic vibrations are highly desirable for trolling because they will sometimes attract a bass from some distance.

Flashy lures. A flashy lure can be seen from some distance, especially in clear water. Shiny spoons and large spinner lures are therefore effective for trolling. My big objection to wobbling spoons and spinners, however, is that they sometimes cause severe line twist.

In many cases, flash can be obtained on sonic lures; Cordell's nickel-plated Spot, for example, is good because it has both flash and sound.

Trolling line. How much line a troller has out can be quite important. Some lines made especially for trolling are marked by color coding every 5 or 10 feet. This is, of course, a big help.

A good trolling line will have low stretch, so that the hook can be set when the lure is some distance out.

Also, some specialized lines are made for deep trolling. A few lines are made of wire, and others have a lead core. I don't think that many bass fishermen use such specialized lines, but if I did a lot of trolling in very deep lakes, I'd certainly check them out. I'd start by reading the manufacturers' literature.

Swivels. My kids and people in my boat have hopelessly twisted a number of monofilament lines while trolling. I've twisted a few myself. One way to reduce line twist is to use a good quality swivel in front of the lure. Remember, however, that high trolling speeds cause pressure on the swivel's bearing surfaces, and the friction tends to make the swivel twist along with the lure. I haven't made any tests, but the consensus these days seems to be that a top-quality ball-bearing swivel works better than a barrel swivel.

Keel sinkers. When a weight is needed to keep a lure working deep, as will often be the case with some lures, I much prefer a keel sinker to a slip sinker or a sinker tied to some sort of three-way swivel. A keel sinker, especially one with good swivels fore and aft, rides upright in the water and thereby helps prevent line twist. Some sinkers, by comparison, will themselves cause line twist. Rubber-core sinkers are especially bad for trolling.

18

Fishing Flies and Bugs

THE BASIC PURPOSE of any rod and reel is to present a lure or bait to a fish at some distance from the angler. A casting outfit is designed to present relatively heavy lures, from ¼ to 1 ounce, depending on the particular outfit and the weight of the line used. The spinning reel and rod are ideal for small lures, from ¹⁄₁₆ to ¼ ounce, although many anglers use heavy line and heavy lures on spinning rigs these days. The fly rod was designed to present featherweight lures—lures that could not possibly be cast unweighted with either bait-casting or spinning gear.

Because most of the fly-rod lures are small as well as light, and because bass (especially largemouth) show a marked preference for large lures (except in cold water), the fly rod, from a purely utilitarian viewpoint, seems to be an unlikely rig for catching black bass.

Moreover, using heavy or large lures on a fly rod presents problems for the angler. In short, the larger and heavier the lure, the more difficult it is to cast on a fly rod. Why? Because a fly rod is designed to cast the *line,* and the lure works against the line. The more weight and the more wind resistance attributed to the lure, the more difficult the cast. Fortunately, however, these difficulties can be overcome, and fairly large bass

159

bugs and flies can be worked effectively with a fly rod. The secret is in careful selection and balance of rod and line.

Why bother when spinning and casting gear can do the job with spoons and plugs and other hardware? Hook a 5-pound bass on a fly rod and you'll know why. More bass anglers ought to try it, though not very many do. A tackle manufacturer told me that fly-rod fishing accounts for only 5 percent of the tackle market, and I would guess that less than 1 percent of bass anglers ever use a fly rod. They are, in my opinion, the elite of bassmen.

But I don't think they have anything to be snobbish about and I don't want to further the impression that fishing with a fly rod requires any special talent or mystique. It doesn't. In fact, it's easier to learn to use a fly-casting outfit—provided that it's well balanced—than to learn to use a bait-casting outfit! Most bass fishermen who were brought up with a bait-casting reel probably won't believe me though.

The only difficult thing in fly casting is making extremely long casts. (There are some fancy casts for various situations, and some of them are difficult to master; these need not concern the bass angler too much, at least not until he becomes quite proficient.) Most bass fishing will require only straightforward casts of 50 feet or less. With the proper equipment, this is a snap.

I'm not going into detail here on how to cast with a fly rod. This information is available in a number of books and can be found in any public library. Many manufacturers of fly-fishing equipment include casting instructions with their rods and reels, and a number of them publish booklets and other fly-casting aids. I especially recommend Scientific Anglers' 50-cent *To Cast a Fly*, Fenwick's $2.00 *Fly Casting from the Beginning*, and Weber's *Fly Fishing Is Easy*.

It is a mistake to buy a fly-rod outfit without first doing some research. And it is definitely a mistake to select at random a cheap outfit for learning purposes. It's not only a waste of money, but it also makes good casting impossible and thus may discourage an angler from pursuing this excellent sport. I strongly recommend that before buying his gear the novice first talk to some expert fly casters and write to several manufacturers of fly-fishing equipment. The better companies may offer personalized guidance in selecting the proper gear for specific fishing conditions; if not, their general catalogs and brochures will be informative. Meanwhile, here are some pointers:

The rod. For casting bass bugs, a rod from 8 to 9 feet long is highly desirable. A longer rod isn't necessary and requires some muscle if you're going to use it all day. A shorter rod won't do the job and requires mismatching the line with the rod in order to get a bass bug out.

I started with an 8½-foot fly rod, which was obtained with S&H Green Stamps. The rod works well enough for casting bluegill bugs, but it leaves something to be desired for casting larger bass bugs any distance. I have now gone to a System 9 Scientific Anglers rod (8 feet 11 inches). It is fairly expensive, but in my opinion it's worth the money to anyone who takes his fishing seriously. Some rods are even more expensive. The Orvis Wes Jordan line, for example, sells for over $200. Although most of the more expensive rods do handle better than most of the inexpensive ones, they are not necessary for a few hours of casual bass fishing. Part of the expense of the better rods is incurred because of the careful wrapping on the guides and tips. And of course the fittings on most of the better rods are top quality. Do-it-yourselfers can save some money by purchasing a quality rod blank and wrapping the guides on them-selves.

Some of the more expensive rods are made of bamboo. A few of these sell for hundreds, even thousands, of dollars, and some connoisseurs say that only the best Tonkin bamboo is acceptable. The fine bamboo rod is truly a thing of beauty, but it may not be a joy forever. The tips of bamboo rods are easy to break, and the rods require great care. If the lacquer chips and the bamboo gets wet, the rod will ultimately weaken at that spot. The glass rods require less attention and will serve the average angler longer. The new high modulus graphite rods are lighter than either bamboo or fiberglass, but they are expensive. The Fenwick graphite fly rods start at about $200.

Most of the more expensive glass rods now have glass-to-glass ferrules, whereas the less expensive models have metal-to-metal ones. The glass ferrules are undeniably better, giving the angler the feeling that the rod is working from tip to butt.

The reel. In most fly fishing, as compared to bait casting and spinning, the reel is of little importance. All the reel does is hold the line. It doesn't turn on the cast and isn't necessary in playing a fish of average size. On the other hand, the reel can become important in fighting a very large fish, and some of the better reels have adjustable drags. Typically, such a reel will be large enough to hold 100 yards of backing line in addition to 30 yards of fly line. I recommend such a reel for bass fishing just in case one ties into a real lunker. I have seldom used my backing line while fishing for bass, but I like to know it's there.

A secondary purpose of the reel is to balance the rod. For this reason, it must be of approximately the right weight for the rod on which it is used.

I prefer a traditional fly reel because I like its simplicity, but some anglers like an automatic reel better. An automatic "picks up" surplus line by a spring-loaded winding mechanism. The automatics are handy, but they are heavier and more likely to cause mechanical problems.

Some of the better reels run up to $40 or more, but generally the reel is not as expensive as the rod. My first one cost me a couple of bucks, and it served me well until I tied into a big gar when fishing a hair rat!

The line. Although the bass angler may economize somewhat on a rod, and even more on a reel, he is wise to purchase a top-quality fly line. My first fly line cost $1.67, and I spent half my fishing time applying line dressing to it in a vain attempt to keep it afloat.

The difficulty in choosing a line is that different rods require different weights of line. And heavy lures require a different line from light lures. Moreover, there are within each weight of line several types, such as floating, sinking, floating/sinking, tapered, level, double-tapered, weight forward. There may still be other line classification systems around, but, thank God, more and more line makers have adopted the American Fishing Tackle Manufacturers Association standards and symbols, established in 1961.

Actually, there are three sets of symbols used to classify a fly line. One set designates the type of line: F for floating, S for sinking, and I for intermediate (floating or sinking). Another set of symbols indicates the taper: L for level, ST for single taper, DT for double-tapered, WF for weight forward. An L line has no taper; its diameter is the same throughout. An ST line is tapered on one end. A DT line is tapered on both ends so that when one end becomes worn (or stepped on too often) the angler can remove the line and reverse it instead of throwing it away. A WF line is heavier toward the end, and this type works better for casting relatively heavy bass bugs.

The other set of symbols, designated by numbers, stands for the weight of the line in grains. Here are the standards:

Number	Weight	Tolerance Range
3	100	94–106
4	120	114–126
5	140	134–146
6	160	152–168
7	185	177–193
8	210	202–218
9	240	230–250
10	280	270–290
11	330	318–342
12	380	368–392

The weight is determined by the first 30 feet of the line, including the tapered part.

Thus, a line labeled WF-6-F would be a weight-forward floating line that weighs from 152 to 168 grains. An L-8-S would be a nontapered sinking line that weighs between 202 and 218 grains. An ST-9-F would be a single-taper floating line that weighs between 230 and 250 grains. And so on.

Actually, the ideal fly-casting outfit—rod, reel, and line—is determined to a large degree by the kind of lure the angler intends to use and how far he wants to cast it. A large bass bug cannot be cast effectively by a line weighing less than 200 grains, and anything heavier than 250 is not needed. This means that a No. 8 or No. 9 line will cast a bass bug effectively. As it happens, it takes an 8- or 9-foot rod to handle lines of this weight. (However, the numbers do *not* indicate rod length; obviously, a No. 3 line would require a rod longer than 3 feet.) Choosing a No. 8 line for an 8- or 8½-foot rod will usually be about right, but check with the rod makers' recommendations before buying. Rod length isn't the only consideration; a heavy rod (bass action, salmon action, etc.) will require a different line from an ultralight rod.

Clearly, one can make serious mistakes when buying a fly line, and a salesman or salesgirl in a discount store is not likely to be of much help. (In fact, I've seen automatic fly reels put on spinning rods, and spinning reels on saltwater rods as stiff as pool cues!) As stated earlier, the best bet is to consult either an experienced fly fisherman or literature from a reputable manufacturer of fly-fishing equipment.

For most of your bass fishing, you'll need a No. 8 or 9 floating line. It's possible to get by with a level line, which is considerably cheaper than a tapered line. But a weight-forward line is much, much better for long casts, and some firms market a special bass bug taper. A good level line sells for $4.00 to $5.00, whereas a weight-forward line or good bass bug taper sells for $12.00 or $15.00, or more. The difference in performance is well worth the extra cost if you plan to do very much bass fishing, unless you are going to be making only short casts.

The leader. Bass bugs are heavy and highly wind resistant. They therefore require a stiff leader to transmit energy from the fly line to the bug at the end of the cast. A tapered leader works best. It's possible to purchase knotless tapered leaders, but I've never seen one in a tackle shop that was heavy enough for bass bugs. The best bet is to tie your own from different weights of monofilament line (or special leader material).

I use a 7-foot leader made up of 4 feet of 25-pound-test line, 1½ feet of 17-pound line, and 1½ feet of 10-pound line. It is, or can be, impor-

tant that all these leader lines be made from the same brand of monofilament simply because such properties as stiffness and diameter for any
one test vary considerably from brand to brand.

The heavier line (25-pound on my leaders) should be joined to the
fly line and should be of approximately the same stiffness. The best way
to join the leader to the fly line is to use a nail knot, tied as shown in
Figures 75, 76, 77, and 78.

The next weight in the leader (17-pound on my leaders) should be
joined to the heavier monofilament with a blood knot, tied as shown in

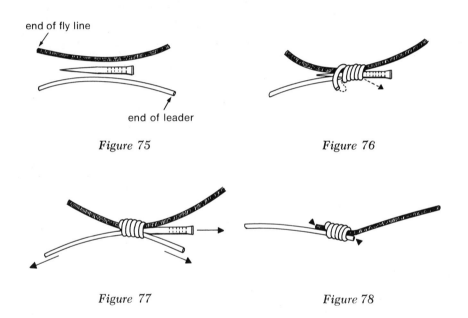

Figure 75   Figure 76

Figure 77   Figure 78

*Figure 75. Hold the end of the fly line, the end of the leader, and the nail beside
one another. (A tube can be used instead of a nail.)*
*Figure 76. Wrap the end of the leader around the nail and fly line six times, and
then run the end of the leader along the nail (or through the tube), as indicated
by the dotted lines and arrow.*
*Figure 77. Pull both ends of the leader material down snugly, and remove the
nail. After the nail is clear, tighten the knot by pulling hard on both ends of the
leather material.*
Figure 78. Trim the ends, as indicated.

Figures 79 through 84. Instructions to tie this knot, keyed to the figure numbers, have been adapted as follows from Du Pont's technical bulletin "Recommended Knots to Use."

Figure 79

Figure 80

Figure 81

Figure 82

Figure 83

Figure 84

Figure 79. Lap the ends of the strands to be joined and twist one around the other, making at least five turns. Count the turns made. Place the ends between the strands, following the arrow.

Figure 80. With thumb and forefinger, hold the end against the turns already made. In other words, hold at the point marked "X" to keep the turns from unwinding. Now wind the other short end around the other strand for the same number of turns, but in the opposite direction.

Figure 81. This is how the knot would look if held firmly in place. Actually, as soon as released, the turns equalize.

Figure 82. The turns look like this after they have equalized. Now pull on both ends of the monofilaments.

Figure 83. As pulling on the ends is continued, the turns gather as above and draw closer together (at this point the short ends may be worked backward, if desired, to avoid cutting off too much of the material).

Figure 84. This is how the finished knot should look. All that remains to be done is to cut off the short ends close to the knot.

Figure 85

The next weight in the leader (10-pound) is joined to the 17-pound line with another blood knot. Then the fly or bug is tied on with an ordinary improved clinch knot or the Palomar knot, as discussed in Chapter 1.

When you are fishing in very clear and shallow water, it's a good idea to go down to a 6-pound tippet, and you may even want a longer leader. I merely tie about 14 inches of 6-pound monofilament onto the end of my standard leaders. Generally, however, bass are not as leader-shy as trout because they don't feed as extensively on tiny insects and larvae.

Most fly rodders use only top-water baits for bass. A surface lure and a floating line are easier to pick up for the back cast, and they are easier to fish in every aspect. Sinking lures can of course be used with a floating line, but they must be fished rather shallow. If you plan to fish deep, you need a sinking line. Orvis—and possibly other firms—has come out with a sinking-tip fly line, and I think this is a good one for fishing depths of 12 or 15 feet.

In any case, the beginner should stick to a floating line until he masters top-water fishing.

One mark of a good trout angler is his ability to match the hatch; that is, he must select a fly that looks like whatever the trout are feeding on at the time. He has hundreds of fly patterns to choose from. The bass fisherman, however, can get by with just a few lures because the bass—especially the largemouth—isn't particular about what it eats. There are exceptions, of course, as when bass are feeding on schooling minnows and won't touch anything else. Most of the time, however, a bassman

Figure 86

needs only a few baits to take bass on a fly rod, although my bug box is getting rather crowded. Here's my breakdown of fly-rod lures:

Popping bugs. These are the favorites, but they may not always be the best. Typically, these bugs have a scooped-out face and should be plunked along in very much the same way as fishing a popping plug with a bait-casting outfit.

One method that sometimes takes bass, especially with bugs having rubber legs, is to fish them "dead" in water with a light chop. The ripples apparently keep the legs moving enticingly. Bugs fished dead in streams can also be effective at times.

Popping bugs come in all colors, and some are painted to look like frogs,

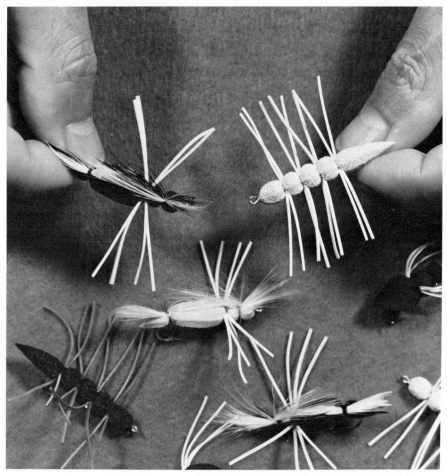

Figure 87

bees, and whatnot. A typical selection is shown in Figure 85. One big mistake that the beginner makes is buying the larger bugs, which are difficult to cast. Start with a size 2 bug, and don't try to cast one larger than 1/0, at least not at first.

Like all other surface lures, popping bugs are more effective around weed beds and lily pads and other cover. The best fishing will be early and late in the day and on overcast days when the bass are more likely to be feeding in shallow water.

Scooting bugs. Instead of having a scooped-out face, these bugs are more streamlined. They are fished very much like popping bugs—twitch and rest, twitch and rest—but they don't cause as much ruckus on the water.

Figure 88

They will sometimes produce better than popping bugs, especially on calm days in clear water.

Hair bugs. These are excellent bass baits, and I prefer them over cork or plastic bugs. They are lighter and easier to cast, although there is a good deal of wind resistance. Some of the more popular bugs in this class include hair frogs and hair mice, as shown in Figure 86.

Sponge-rubber spiders. These baits are among my favorites for bass. As shown in Figure 87, one of their main attractions is the rubber legs. I often fish these fast by stripping in line with foot-long hauls, pausing for a second or two between each haul.

Wet flies. I feel that too many bass anglers neglect wet flies. I usually

Figure 89

Figure 90

fish them in shallow water, at the edge of weed beds or treetops. When unweighted, they sink slowly, and I watch my fly line very, very closely. A slight twitch may indicate that a bass has engulfed the lure. After a fly sinks a couple of feet or more, I fish it along by making 6- or 8-inch hauls. Then I pause a second or two between each haul.

There are all manner of wet flies, and most of them will catch bass. My favorites are the Wooly Worms (Figure 88) and the Muddler Minnow types. The various streamer flies, Figure 89, are also good.

I've also had good luck with Best's Stanley Streamer, Figure 90. These have a plastic lip, which makes them dart about in the water. They have more wiggle than regular streamers, but they are more difficult to pick up for the back cast. I dart these along a little faster than a regular streamer, and I usually fish them with the rod tip instead of by hauling in line.

Frankly, I don't use a fly rod for bass as often as I use bait-casting and spinning gear. But I do thoroughly enjoy it, and I have at times used flies to outfish pluggers and even wormsters.

Just the other day, for example, I went out to catch fifteen bluegills for supper. I had them within thirty minutes, but of course I didn't come right in. After catching and releasing a few more bluegills, I tied on a No. 2 Wooly Worm to try for bass. I was fishing along a grass bed running parallel to the bank. A couple of guys who were trolling for bass nearby had seen that I was catching fish, although I don't think they knew that the fish were bluegills.

Anyhow, just after I had tied on the Wooly Worm, they quit trolling, tied on plastic worms, and started fishing the weed bank just ahead of my boat. Well, this didn't set just right with me, but I fished along behind them. Soon a 2½-pound bass took the Wooly Worm, and I played the fish much longer than necessary, putting on a show for the intruders.

After that, we fished along for a few minutes without any action in either boat. Next, I hooked into a smaller bass, about a pound, and let him jump a couple of times before boating him. By now the boat ahead had slowed down and was only 15 yards ahead of me.

"What are you using?" one of the guys asked, cranking in his plastic worm.

"A Wooly Worm," I said.

"Huh?"

"A Wooly Worm wet fly. I'm trying to catch some bluegills, but these old bass keep grabbing it."

The intruder clammed up, and, without pushing my luck further, I cranked the kicker and headed home. I'll have to admit that I felt a little superior to those bait casters—those *worm* fishermen—and I fear that I may be in danger of becoming a fly-rod snob!

Part Four

Fishing
with
Lunker Bait

19

Catching the Shiner

ACCORDING TO AN ARTICLE in *Florida Wildlife*, an Alabamian fishing in Lake Jackson weighed in two bass that tipped the scales a hair over 14 pounds each. And before he boated the first one, he had tied into six others that broke his 20-pound line! Like many other fishermen who go after lunkers with live bait, he was using golden shiners. But he had 10-inch shiners, whereas most fishermen settle for 4- to 6-inchers. It's no secret that the larger shiners will catch the larger bass, but the problem is in obtaining 8- to 12-inchers.

At one time, commercial "shiner men" caught and sold the larger shiners to bass fishermen in some areas. Most of these shiner men used circular cast nets, but a few used a hook and line. I remember buying shiners years ago from an old hook-and-liner on the St. Johns River. He sold them right at his shiner hole, directly from a large live well built into his weathered cypress boat. They were 10 cents each. Although I have recently heard of large wild shiners going for as high as 75 cents each, virtually all the shiners that are sold today are hatchery raised, and nearly all bait dealers handle only the small or medium-sized ones. There are exceptions, but they are very few.

Unless you hire a big-bass guide who provides large shiners for his customers, about the only way to obtain them is to catch your own. This is certainly no cinch. As in most other forms of fishing, the secret of taking shiners consistently is to have the right tackle, use the right bait, and fish in the right place.

The tackle should be light. I use a No. 16 hook, a 4-pound monofilament line, and a 1-inch cigar-shaped float, as shown in Figure 91. If I use a sinker at all, it is very small. A limber cane or fiberglass pole is ideal, and I have even used a fly rod. A short-shank "salmon egg" hook will probably take more shiners, but I prefer a long shank because

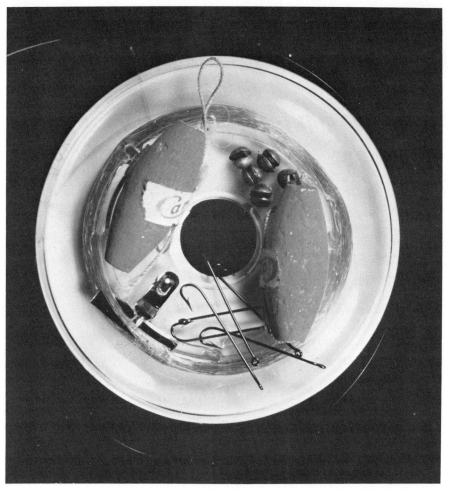

Figure 91

it is easier to remove from the shiner's mouth, resulting in less injury and handling. (Some purists even use a barbless hook.) An injured shiner will die quickly, and a dead shiner won't often attract big bass. I also find a small landing net to be useful, not only because large shiners often pull off if they are lifted from the water, but also because a netted shiner won't be as likely to get loose and flop around in the boat.

Shiner bait should be small, because a shiner has a small mouth. I normally use little BB-sized pills of ordinary white bread. The fresher the better. This bait is prepared by removing the soft core of a slice of bread and kneading it into a ball. Then individual baits are pinched off. The bait keeps better if the large ball is kept in a plastic bag or wrapped in foil.

I'm not saying, however, that white bread is the best possible shiner bait. Some people prefer dough balls of various concoction, and others use a gook made of moistened oatmeal. I use white bread because it is convenient and not messy. But if the shiners don't bite the bread, I switch to natural baits, such as a piece of worm or small crickets. Once I took shiners on mayflies when they wouldn't touch anything else!

Generally, shiners bite best in early morning and late afternoon. But I've caught them at all hours of the day and even at night.

Since golden shiners and subspecies are widely distributed from coast to coast, there are bound to be habitat variations from place to place, season to season. Basically, however, shiners are schooling fish. They like to cruise along grass beds that are adjacent to deeper water. I don't think that a depth finder and other electronic gadgets will be necessary to locate shiners on most lakes, but the fisherman may have to move about quite a bit to find a good shiner spot.

By far the best bet is to use chum. Since shiners do roam about, they'll find bait in almost any suitable spot. Sometimes they'll come in overnight, but it is wise to chum several areas at least two days in advance. I use scrap bread or wet oatmeal for chum, and I simply cast it out. If the bread is very dry, I work it in water so that it will sink instead of drifting off.

After shiners start coming to a chum area, they'll churn the water violently for floating bread or oatmeal. I often catch as many as I need by fishing about 6 inches deep in a swarm of surface-feeding shiners. The competition for the chum will turn an otherwise persnickety shiner into a voracious feeder! When the chum is on the bottom, however, or when you are fishing without chum, it is best to go down 4 feet deep or even deeper. But don't fish right on the bottom.

If an angler plans to use a lot of large shiners—or wants a few quickly—

a circular cast net would be a good investment. When you are using a cast net, it is important that you get the shiners feeding on the surface before you throw the net. Some sort of floating chum, such as oatmeal or dry bread, works best. Remember that you'll have to catch all the shiners on the first cast, simply because the net sends them off in a panic. It is important, therefore, that you learn to use the cast net unerringly.

As already indicated, it is difficult to keep large wild shiners alive. At least in this respect, the hatchery shiners are much better than the wild kind. For one thing, the more-placated hatchery shiners don't try to jump out of a container at every opportunity, whereas a ray of daylight will cause the wild shiners to either jump out or kill themselves trying. I've had them jump clean out of the boat! Generally, they'll do less jumping and fare better all around if they are kept still in a dark, cool place.

Frankly, I've never found a really ideal container for keeping large wild shiners. Maybe it's impossible. For a while I used large styrofoam ice chests, which are probably the best containers in which to keep the shiners alive, but I too often had too many shiners flopping around on the bottom of the boat. It's difficult to take a shiner out of an ice chest without letting one or more jump out.

I'm currently using a 24-gallon Bait Saver, as shown in Figure 92. Designed primarily for live mullet (which are frequently used to catch tarpon and snook), this container looks like a plastic garbage can, is big enough, and has an efficient small-bubble aerator. The splash-proof lid has a hinged cutout for removing shiners, and I find that by using a small trout-size landing net I can usually dip up one shiner at a time and don't have to scramble all over the boat for it.

I also drop large shiners over the side of the boat in a large net bag. Netcraft makes one 60 inches long with 12-inch spreader rings, and it has a C-clamp on the top frame so that it can be easily attached to the boat, as shown in Figure 92. The biggest drawback with such a live net is that it must be taken out of the water when the boat is moved faster than a crawl. My solution is to use the net in conjunction with the Bait Saver. Simply lift the net—shiners and all—and put it into the container until the boat is stopped on bass waters. Then put the net back over the side. When you are switching back and forth, however, remember to avoid appreciable changes in temperature.

Unless you do equip yourself to keep large wild shiners and take the necessary precautions, you are better off buying the tamer hatchery kind. At many bait outlets, you can purchase shiners in plastic, oxygen-inflated bags, which will keep bait in good shape even overnight. There is no doubt

Figure 92

that the hatchery shiners are much easier to keep and handle, and there is no doubt that lively hatchery shiners will catch more bass than dead wild shiners. There's nothing more disheartening than to spend half your lunker fishing time catching bait—only to end up at your favorite bass hole with a bucketful of belly-up shiners.

On the other hand, a 12-inch shiner puts up a pretty good fight if taken on light tackle, so that catching the bait can be fun in itself. Shiners are edible, too, and I've heard of some anglers who go after them, for sport and food, with small spinners and trout flies. I've never fished for shiners in this manner, but the largest one I've ever seen took a small popping bug while I was fly rodding for bluegills. This big shiner put up a memorable battle—and was delicious, even if a little bony!

20

Rigging Up

ONCE I KNEW a very nice retired broker who fished large shiners on a Florida lake almost daily for nearly a year before he finally caught a bass impressive enough to weigh. It barely tipped the scales at 5 pounds, and he couldn't understand how I kept bringing in 10-pounders, using the same bait on the same lake. The reason was that I knew more about largemouth bass and therefore knew that I had to be more painstaking. More careful. More fussy. I also took my fishing more seriously.

My friend made several mistakes. First, he too often fished where few bass were. Second, he eased the line tight when he did happen to get a bite, as though afraid that he would stick the hook into a bass. Third, his shiners were not kept lively. Fourth, he stood up to fish, wore loud clothing and white hats, banged around in his boat, and generally made his presence known. Fifth, he used too much terminal tackle.

After chain pickerel started cutting his 8-pound monofilament line, he went up to 15-pound and then, in steps, all the way up to 60-pound. Moreover, he started using those nylon-clad wire leaders. He used three-way swivels, eyelet-swivel sinkers, and all manner of hardware, including a snap swivel (safety pin) on the end of his line to make it more convenient to change hooks.

180

There are no doubt applications for all this tackle, but the way to catch big bass with shiners is to keep the rig as simple as possible. Eliminate all unnecessary hardware. In some situations, all you need is a hook and line. In others, you'll need a sinker to take the shiner down or a float to keep it up. It's as simple as that. But remember that one float is not as good as another, one line is not as good as another, one hook is not as good as another, and one sinker is not as good as another.

The line. I usually use a top-quality 25-pound-test line for shiner fishing. I'll use a 30-pound line over submerged brush or in other tight spots. I'll also use a 30-pound line on the rather rare occasions when I fish with a cane pole in potholes, as in an opening in water hyacinths. About 95 percent of the time I use monofilament instead of braided line. When I do use braided line, it's the floating kind, and its application will be explained more fully in Chapter 21.

The hook. I prefer a single-barb hook to a treble. The single barb digs in deeper and holds better. The hook I use is stout, has a short shank, and is kept very, very sharp. My preference is the Mustad Salmon hook because it has a long tapered point that more easily penetrates the tough parts of a bass's bony mouth.

Provided that the hook is approximately the right size, the main thing to remember is that its point must be sharp. I always sharpen a new hook, and I keep it honed. Normally, I use a small Arkansas whetstone, and I find that the best edge is produced by pulling the hook point into the stone, at an angle of course, rather than sliding it over the stone or grinding it with a circular motion. I also sharpen the point on the barb of the hook, so that it will bite in and hold. This is best done with a flat-surfaced jeweler's file.

The size of the hook I use varies with the size of the shiner, but I usually prefer a size 4/0 (Mustad Salmon) for 8- and 9-inch shiners and a size 5/0 for very large shiners. The reason I use such a large size is that I normally hook the shiner through the back, under the dorsal fin. The other two commonly used methods of hooking a shiner—through the lips and just above the tail—require a smaller hook because it doesn't have to go through so much meat. But I seldom use either of these methods because, for one thing, a shiner tends to sling off on the cast or else work loose after long use.

I do, however, hook a shiner through the mouth from time to time, usually when I want to fish moderately deep without a sinker. A shiner so hooked tends to run deeper than one hooked through the back or through the tail. I like this method of hooking a shiner, but my main objection to it is that I doubt that the shiner emits as much "stuff" as when hooked through the back. Let me explain.

Some fish sense their food partly by smelling and tasting chemical substances that spread to them through the water from the bait. Exactly what these chemicals are has not been determined, although amino acids (which are components of proteins) are probably an ingredient.

At the University of the West Indies, in Kingston, Jamaica, some scientists experimented with a small fish of the Caribbean, named *Bathystema rimater*. They found that the fish went "food hunting" when extracts of certain animal tissues were diffused in the water. Extracts from a sea urchin, two crustaceans, a worm, a sea cucumber, and a squid all brought on feeding reactions from the fish.

More recent research at other places tends to indicate that freshwater bait fish, such as shiners and shad, also emit some such substance when they are wounded or hooked. I don't have any evidence, but I suspect that a shiner emits more of this substance when it is hooked through the back than when hooked through the mouth, where the hook penetrates mostly through some sort of cartilaginous tissue.

I have heard that some fishermen who specialize in fishing for large bass hook shiners through the tail with a treble hook. I've tried this, but I tend to sling off too many good shiners on the cast. And, personally, I've never seen any advantage in using a treble hook.

The float. I've always thought that people who manufacture fishing tackle are thinking of fishermen instead of fish when they make floats red and white or other bright colors. True, the colors make the floats easier for the fishermen to see. But they also make them easier for the bass to see, and I've always believed that one has a better chance of fooling a lunker bass if it can see only the bait or the lure.

A couple of years ago I made an experiment that tends to bear out my thinking. My wife and I had just moved to our place on Timucuan Island, and we were doing some shiner fishing. I painted my float green and left hers red and white. I caught the fish. The next time out, she used the green float, and she caught more fish than I did. Although I didn't run the experiment long enough to collect anything like scientific data, the evidence was strong enough to convince me to paint all our floats green!

Since then I've gone to brown and other solid colors, but I can't tell any difference between them and green. And I really don't think that a red-and-white float will scare a bass. I've seen too many bass strike at them in choppy water! I do think, though, that a loud, two-toned float, such as red and white, may look unnatural and therefore may cause old grandpa bass to be a bit more wary. I might add that a float is more noticeable in shiner fishing than in some other forms of fishing because the shiner, if it is lively, keeps the float moving.

Before painting just any old float, it pays to give some thought to the shape, size, and design. I dislike those plastic-bubble spring-loaded clip-on floats on several counts. One big reason is that they are round. An egg-shaped float is better, but my favorite is cigar-shaped because it has less water and wind resistance. I don't want old grandpa bass to be worried by any more resistance than necessary when he bites and runs with my shiner, and I don't want my shiner pulling around any more than is neces-sary. Also, a cigar-shaped float is better for fishing in strong wind, which can at times be an important consideration. When two shiners are fished from the same boat in windy weather, they tend to drift with the wind and end up a few feet apart behind the boat. With cigar-shaped floats, the shiner can swim against the wind easier.

The exact size of a float isn't too critical, but it must be large enough to prevent the shiner from taking it underwater for any length of time. I use balsa cigar floats from 5 to 10 inches long, and my rule of thumb is to have the float as long as the shiner.

Instead of clipping on, most of the cigar floats have a hollow core. The better ones are reamed out and fitted with a plastic or metal tube through which the line goes. A wood plug comes with most floats, along with directions to insert the plug into the hole to bind the line, thereby keeping the float in place. I normally don't use a plug because it prevents me from winding the line in past the point where the float is attached. This im-pedes casting and limits the depth at which one can fish with such a rig. (In other words, if you had a float fixed 20 feet from the hook, how would you cast the rig out? How would you get a bass in?)

Without the plug, the float will slip up and down the line. This makes casting easier because the float slides down to the sinker or hook and the whole works can be reeled right up to the rod tip. The depth of the shiner can be regulated with a bead and a knotted piece of rubber band. The rubber band is tied tightly around the line with a simple overhand knot. The ends are clipped off. Then the bead is threaded on. The float, sinker, and hook are put on next. When cast out, the shiner moves off and the float slides up the line to the bead, which in turn slides up the line until it reaches the rubber band. A knot in the line can be used instead of the rubber band, but some knots reduce the strength of mono-filament drastically. Besides, a knot in the line fixes the depth until it is untied, whereas a rubber band can be slipped up and down the line to vary the depth. The rubber-band knot, if clipped properly, goes smoothly through rod guides and can be wound onto the reel spool with either casting or spinning gear. The only trouble that I have had with the rubber-band rig is that it sometimes comes undone or else it slips. The better the quality of the rubber, the tighter the knot can be drawn down without breaking the band.

I have also used small plastic devices called bobber stoppers, and they work very well. The only trouble with these is that I lose them too easily in my tackle box! (My beads also have a way of getting away from me.) Anyhow, the gadget looks like a tiny bone with a hole in either end. The line is run through the end, wrapped around the center, and run out the other end, as shown in Figure 93. When tightened down, the line and the bobber stopper go easily through rod guides and onto the spool of the reel. Like the rubber band, the bobber stopper can be slid up and down the line to adjust the shiner's depth.

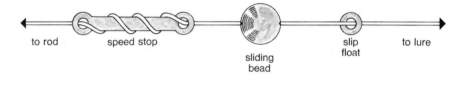

to rod   speed stop   slip   to lure
                                                              float
                                    sliding
                                    bead

Figure 93

The plastic device I use is made by the Arnold Tackle Corporation. A similar device, or one that serves the same purpose, is made by Fin, a subsidiary of Fred Arbogast Company. It is a spring made of soft wire. The line is run through the center of the spring, and then the spring is stretched from both ends, which tightens it down on the line. This device can be pushed up or down the line to adjust the depth, and it can be wound onto the reel spool. It works fine.

When using either the rubber band or a bobber stopper device, you have a rig that is easy to cast and can be fished at any depth. I have fished such rigs from 3 to 35 feet deep, and I see no reason why they can't be fished even deeper if desirable.

The sinker. Ideally, I prefer no sinker at all because I think they impede a shiner's action, tire it out, and limit its range. But I always use a sinker when I want to fish very deep, simply because the shiner won't go down without being weighted. I've had 20 feet of line between the float and the hook, only to find that the shiner would be nosing about on the surface!

For convenience, I sometimes use rubber-core sinkers. The line is run through the slot in the lead. Then the rubber "ears" on either end of the sinker are twisted 180 degrees, taking the line around with it. Thus it's very easy to put a sinker on or take it off without having to cut off the hook. My only objection to rubber-core sinkers is that they are too large for their weight, or too light for their size, which ever way you look at it. Of course, I'm thinking about how the *bass* may look at it.

I generally avoid using any kind of split-shot or squeeze-on sinker because I don't want to pinch it onto my monofilament line.

If I'm going to fish extremely deep with a sinker, I'll put on an egg-shaped slip sinker. To rig it, I first cut about 30 inches off the end of my line. Then I insert the main line through the sinker and tie it to a small swivel or split ring. Finally, I tie the 30-inch line on and attach a hook.

Whether or not I use a sinker, and how heavy it is, depends almost entirely on the depth I want to fish, which in turn depends on the time of day and other conditions related to the habits and ways of largemouth bass. Sinkers definitely have a place in fishing with large shiners for big bass. But, day in and day out, you'll have a better chance of catching a real trophy if it doesn't *have* to take hook, line, and sinker. Hook and line will do.

21

Fishing the Shiner

A GOOD MANY ANGLERS look down their noses at shiner fishermen, and most outdoor writers treat the subject condescendingly and apologetically. The general opinion of such people is that live bait is a last resort, to be used only when the bass aren't hitting artificials. Some expert angling writers concede that the large shiner is the best bet for catching a trophy bass— and then proceed to give bad advice. Recently, for example, an angling writer said that if he were after a world's record largemouth, he would fish a shiner off one side of the boat and cast artificials off the other side.

The truth is that fishing a large shiner properly is a full-time job. A large shiner in lively condition is constantly coming back to the boat or getting tangled in the cover or going away from the cover. A shiner will swim all about the boat, 360 degrees. Liveliness is what makes the shiner such good lunker bait, but fishing them can be quite exasperating.

And shiner fishing is not for everybody. It's slow. Day in and day out, the shiner man gets fewer strikes and catches fewer pounds of bass than the competent plugger or the expert fly fisherman. In short, fishing a large shiner can be a bore—but not to me, because I always remember my first experience with large shiners.

While fishing for bluegills, I caught a huge shiner, which I knew to be good lunker bait. Deciding to try it, I rigged with a bass hook and a big cork float. To be honest, I was almost afraid to throw the shiner out. I was only thirteen years old, and I was fishing alone in a 10-foot homemade boat. The shiner must have weighed almost a pound, and I knew that anything I hooked into would have to be almost big enough to pull the boat under!

For two hours I had no action. Then, suddenly, the shiner became very lively and jerked the float about. Twice the shiner jumped completely out of the water. Then the float popped under, and it didn't come up. The line straightened out. The reel spool turned. Fast. I knew that the moment of truth was upon me: I was about to tangle with my first lunker bass.

I set the hook hard, and the bass jerked the reel handle out of my hand. (That was back in the days when casting reels had no drag mechanism.) After busting my knuckles, I managed to get my thumb on the spool. The bass kept going, doggedly, toward the middle of the lake. I never even turned it.

If I were to tie into that bass today and it headed for open water, I would have a much better chance of putting it into the boat. I would, for one thing, have 100 yards of good line on my reel. I would also have a good drag. And, if I had to, I would either get the anchor up or cut the line and follow the bass with my foot-controlled electric motor!

Although a fishing partner can be a big help in getting anchor lines in, many shiner men prefer to fish alone. I am one of them, for several reasons. First, one large shiner fished off one boat is enough; two or more lively shiners will have to be reeled in often to keep them out of each other's way, and too much reeling in and casting out will maim the bait. Second, it is, in my opinion, important that the shiner fisherman be very quiet. And still. I don't want anybody stomping around in the boat or clanking tackle boxes shut or slinging artificial lures around when I'm fishing a shiner. I don't want anybody wearing a white shirt or standing up in the boat. Third, shiner fishing is a slow go, and I don't want anybody discouraging me with talk about the fish not biting. My wife says that I'm too fussy—and maybe I am. But I'm certain that it pays to be careful when fishing shiners, especially when you will be fishing the same spot for an hour or more.

Although I don't want any boat noises, I feel that a shiner splashing down in the water at the end of a cast may attract bass, and I've caught several lunkers shortly after my shiner hit down. For this reason, I prefer to cast a shiner out. But many experienced fishermen seldom cast shiners because it hurts them. They put them in the water at the boat and let them swim out, or else they drop them off the side and move the boat away. I generally use this method when I have only one or two shiners. But if I've got plenty of bait, I cast them out. On the other hand, I don't like to cast out too often, and I am sometimes aggravated by a fool shiner that keeps running back to the boat. This is often a problem. Sometimes, when a shiner heads back to the boat or runs in a direction that is otherwise undesirable, you can turn it around by pulling in a couple of feet of line.

In addition to banging up the bait, another hazard in casting is that a backlash, a bird's nest, or an improper cast can sling or jerk the shiner off the hook. You can't really cast a big shiner with a flick of the wrist; it has to be slung out. Proper equipment will help, but anybody will lose a large shiner from time to time, especially when trying to make long casts. A large shiner is heavy, and it is difficult to cast with a limber rod.

My favorite shiner-fishing outfit is a medium-sized saltwater spinning reel with an 8-foot, rather stiff rod. This size rod works nicely when casting the shiner, when setting the hook, and when fighting a lunker bass. One big advantage in the large spinning reel is that it spools 25- or 30-pound monofilament better than smaller freshwater spinning reels.

I almost always use spinning gear and monofilament line, but there is one exception when I switch to a casting rig and braided line. The trouble with monofilament is that it sinks, and this can cause difficulties when you're fishing over moss, submerged grass, stumps, or otherwise cluttered bottom. Not too long ago, for example, I was shiner fishing when a bass popped my float under. I let the bass run for a few seconds, then tried to set the hook. But I didn't stick the bass. Although I thought I had all the slack out before I tried to set the hook, the line had settled down around some moss directly off the side of the boat. I thought the bass was running that way, but it was actually going around the bow of the boat! When I tried to set the hook, I merely jerked the line off the moss, thereby ending up with a lot of slack line. And no bass. The float surfaced off the bow.

If I had been using a floating line, it wouldn't have fouled on the bottom and I would have known which way the bass was running. A floating line also lets the angler see when all the slack is taken up, which can be a problem with monofilament because a running bass can strip line off the spool long before all the slack is out, owing to the drag of the line in the water. I've never found an ideal floating line, but I have been using Cortland's Heart-O-Gold, a line that was made for fishing top-water plugs. I keep it treated with a good fly-line dressing.

I usually prefer to fish with monofilament, and a lively shiner can keep it up off the bottom if the angler watches his business and takes in slack

instead of casting artificials off the other side of the boat. But in shallow
water—5 feet or less—I prefer to use the floating line, especially over
weedy or mossy bottom. Even when I do use a braided line, I always
tie on a 25-pound monofilament leader.

There are several ways to fish a shiner. One of the easiest is to let the
boat drift with the wind, but, as with most other easy ways to fish, drifting is not the most productive way. An angler's chances of catching a
lunker are considerably improved if he knows how deep the water is and
what's on the bottom, so that he can adjust the depth of his shiner accordingly. Knowledge of the depth and bottom also permits the fisherman
to choose certain areas instead of drifting blindly across the lake.

When you're drifting in windy weather, it's best to use a clip-on float
or otherwise fix the float to the line. A slip float will tend to work down
to the shiner, and both will be dragged across the top of the water. In
effect, drifting in a stiff breeze is really trolling, in which case the best
method is to hook the shiner through the lips and put a sinker about 20
inches above the hook.

Another way to fish a shiner is to anchor the boat near some likely spot.
I much prefer this method to drifting. If I am fishing alone, I drop only
one anchor when the wind is blowing steadily from one direction. There's
always the danger of a lunker getting tangled around an anchor line,
and two anchors increase the probability. If the wind is steady, I prefer
to drop the anchor off the stern and let out lots of line. Then I lower
the foot-controlled electric motor off the bow. I fish from the front seat,
and if I tie into a lunker that wants to run toward the anchor line, I
jockey the boat for position.

But when the wind blows first one way and then another, I drop both
bow and stern anchors and keep the lines short. I also tighten my drag
considerably so that I can horse a lunker away from the anchor line. A
long, stout rod also helps.

When two or more people are fishing out of the boat, I almost always
prefer to drop both anchors, lower the electric, and raise the outboard.
As soon as one person ties into a lunker, the other should immediately
take up both anchors.

In many cases, I prefer to keep the boat in position with the electric
motor instead of dropping anchor. In fact, I often more or less follow my
shiner, as long as it wants to go where I think a bass might be. One of
my favorite methods is to position the boat about 20 yards away from a
grass bed, lily pads, or some similar cover and try to work the shiner
down it slowly. In other words, I move the boat parallel to the line of

cover. But this usually requires a good deal of reeling in and casting out, which is rough on bait.

Because shiners are so difficult to control with rod and reel, some fishermen use long cane poles and heavy line. This not only makes it easier to control the shiner, but it also allows the fisherman to pick the shiner up and put it down gently. I see the advantage all right, but, on the other hand, I prefer to fish my shiners farther out than the reach of a pole, especially in clear water. However, a lot of trophy bass are caught on cane poles, and they are ideal for fishing shiners in small openings in thick lily pads and water hyacinths.

You can often tell when you are about to get a bite. The shiner will be more lively than usual, jerking the float around or even taking it under the water. Sometimes a lunker bass will cause a shiner to jump like a mullet. Whenever you see your shiner in panic, get ready. A large bass will usually pop the float under and run fast. When this happens, I get the slack out of my line as quickly as I can. Then I let the bass take line for a few seconds. After I am sure that the line is straight, I set the hook hard.

Most shiner fishermen let a bass run much longer than I do. They want the bass to swallow the bait and the hook, but I try to prevent this. I feel that a gut-hooked lunker will abrade line more than one hooked in the jaw. Ideally, the bass should chomp down on the hook's shank instead of on the line.

Usually, I can tell by the bite whether it's a bass or some other fish, such as chain pickerel or bowfin. A lunker bass, having a large mouth, will take the shiner and go. Pickerel and bowfin tend to piddle around more, often taking the float down and letting it come back up. But I have been fooled, and I recently took an 11-pound largemouth that never even sank the float!

22
Other Live Baits

ONE DAY MY BROTHER was fishing a quiet nook of a small natural lake when a 2-foot green snake tried to climb into the boat. He knocked the snake off, but it came right back. He knocked it off again, but right back it came. Tiring of this, my brother picked the snake up and flung it out about 20 yards. He should have stuck a hook in it because a lunker bass grabbed it on its way back to the boat!

Bass will feed on almost anything that swims in the water or almost any live thing that falls into the water, including birds and mice. I doubt that many people fish with birds or mice or snakes, but they do fish with a wide variety of live baits in one part of the country or another.

Although I recommend live shiners as the best bait, here are some others you may want to try:

Frogs. At times live frogs can be very good bass bait, and I have fished with them in all sizes up to full-grown bullfrogs. I hook them through the lips and cast them out without a float or sinker, but they can also be hooked through the skin of the leg. In my opinion, frogs are more effective when bass are in shallow water. They are especially good at sunup and sundown and when fished among lily pads and such places where a hungry bass would have frogs on its mind.

The best way to obtain live frogs for fishing is to shine them at night with a spotlight and catch them with your hands. You can usually find a few frogs along the bank of any lake or stream in spring, summer, and early autumn, but in my experience they are much more plentiful in ditches and field ponds where there are no bass to eat them.

One very good thing about frogs is that they are easy to keep alive. I keep them in a bag made from nylon netting, but any mesh onion or orange bag will do. I keep the bag wet but not submerged in water. I also put some moss, water hyacinths, or similar stuff in the bag. I've kept frogs several days, but there is a limit to how long they will keep in lively condition. It's best to catch them the night before a fishing trip. If you do spend half the night catching frogs, keep them in a cool, safe place. Once I left a dozen nice ones in the water's edge beside the boat. When I got up at the crack of dawn, thinking I could catch a lunker before sunup, I discovered that a raccoon had torn the bag open and all my bait was gone!

Salamanders and eels. Various kinds of salamanders, known as water dogs, mud puppies, spring lizards, and who knows what else, are probably more important than most anglers realize in a bass's diet. I think that the salamanders, eels, and leeches—not the earthworm—are responsible for the popularity and success of the soft plastic worm.

There are dozens and dozens of various kinds of salamander, and some of them grow 3 feet long. This variety is described in A *Field Guide to Reptiles and Amphibians of Eastern North America:* "North America (including Central America) not only has more varieties of salamanders than all the rest of the world put together, but it boasts an assortment of big bizarre kinds that look more like bad dreams than live animals. Some are long, dark, and slender and resemble eels. Some permanently retain the larval form, bearing external gills throughout their lives. Others are flattened and smack of weird creatures crawling forth from the antediluvian slime. Since all are aquatic and nocturnal, few persons other than fishermen ever meet them in person." I would add that not too many modern anglers meet them either.

I've heard about large catches of bass being made on "lizards" in the Carolinas. Although I don't see why a lizard (reptile) wouldn't make pretty good bait, Carolinians are actually using salamanders, which are sold in some local bait shops.

I've caught a lot of salamanders in wet spots and springs, usually under or in rotting logs. There are so many various kinds of salamanders and newts throughout the country, however, that I can't attempt to discuss all of them and the ways to catch them. If you are serious about this type of bait, you should obtain a good field guide to amphibians and study the habits and range of the various kinds of salamanders. In addition, inquire locally about the best methods of catching these creatures. If you asked about this in the St. Johns River area, for example, you might be told to dip up a large water hyacinth in a landing net and hold it over the bait bucket. If a siren is there, it will often drop right into the bucket! But this technique might be useless in other places.

Eels are, of course, a type of fish, not a type of amphibian, but I include them here with salamanders because of their similarities. Although commercial fishermen can sometimes net eels by the ton, I've never been able to find a good way to catch them for bait. I've caught a number of large eels on hooks, and I've seen (and could catch) thousands of 2½-inch elvers below dams, but I've caught very few from 8 to 12 inches long, which in my opinion would be the best size for large bass. They can, however, be caught in streams with hook and line. It's best to chum a hole for several days, then fish with bits of worm or meat on a small hook. Generally, you can catch more eels at night than during the day.

Crayfish. Although crayfish have been highly touted as bass bait, I seldom use them because I like a faster-moving, swimming bait. I feel that I have a better chance of catching a lunker largemouth on shiners or frogs or sirens. But crayfish will catch lots of bass in some spots—especially smallmouth and spotted bass. It's best to fish them on the bottom without a weight or a float, although a sinker will sometimes be necessary.

Crayfish shed their shells about eight times a year. Unlike the old hard shell, the new one is soft and thereby allows the crayfish to grow. Called peelers, the soft-shell crayfish are generally believed to be much better bait.

Crayfish can be purchased at some bait dealers, but most anglers catch their own. They can be taken in traps, pulled out of shallow ponds and ditches with garden rakes, or even caught by fishing for them (they'll hang onto bait like crabs). They are more active at night and can be caught in shallow water by spotting them with a strong flashlight. In daytime, they tend to run under rocks or banks, at which time I've caught thousands of them by jogging a hoe upstream from a small net or seine.

I've kept crayfish in damp burlap bags, but it's better to keep them in damp moss or grass. They will usually die if kept in minnow-bucket water, especially if they are crowded. They should be kept cool.

Hellgrammites. The larvae of the dobsonfly, hellgrammites live under rocks in fairly swift-moving streams. They grow 3 or 4 inches long and look like creatures from Mars. But they catch bass and are especially good for the smallmouth.

Hellgrammites can be caught by holding a small net or seine immediately below rocks in swift streams; dislodging the rock will cause the hellgrammites to be swept downstream into the net. They should be stored in cool, wet moss or similar material instead of being kept in water like minnows.

In my opinion, hellgrammites are more effective in streams than in lakes. They should be fished just off the bottom, using a small float but no sinker. In streams, let them drift along with the current.

Crickets and grasshoppers. Both these baits will catch bass, especially smallmouth in small streams. But I seldom use them when I'm after a bass because they attract too many bluegills and other panfish. They also catch a lot of trout in some streams.

Minnows and other fish. Although most bass anglers use live shiners, a number of minnows are good bait. In Florida, for example, the Caledonian minnow is excellent bait, but, like most other minnows, it doesn't grow large enough to suit me. Shad are good bait too, but, in my experience, they are almost impossible to keep alive.

Bluegills, redear, pumpkinseed, crappie, and similar panfish will catch lunker bass. I have had several big bass attack bluegills when I was playing them on a fly rod. But I'm sure that bass would rather have a shiner to eat. Bluegills and their cousins have sharp, stout fins, which make them difficult to swallow. There's no denying, though, that bass feed on bream, and I've seen more than one lunker floating dead with a bluegill stuck in its gullet. When I do use bream, I rig and fish them like I do shiners. (Before using bluegills and similar fish for bait, be sure to check the game laws in your state.)

Small catfish are also good bass bait, and they are a good deal easier to keep alive than shiners. In some areas the tadpole madtom, a small catfish, is highly prized as smallmouth bait. When you are fishing with larger bullheads and catfish, it's best to snip their spines.

Worms. Various kinds of earthworms are excellent bait, especially for smaller bass. I've caught and released a hundred 1- and 2-pound bass during a morning's fishing with worms. I prefer to fish worms with a light 14-foot cane pole and 16 feet of monofilament line, without float or sinker. But worms can be fished successfully with casting or spinning gear.

Although worms are excellent bait for smaller bass, I seldom use them when I'm after a lunker. Even so, very large bass have been known to take them. On June 23, 1973, for example, an angler caught a 20-pound, 15-ounce largemouth in Lake Miramar, California, on a live night crawler!

Part Five

When
and
Where to Fish

23

Impoundments and Lakes

By far the hottest bass fishing available to the average angler is in the large new man-made impoundments. Whatever the detrimental or beneficial effects on the total environment may be, the new impoundments have consistently provided bass bonanza after bass bonanza around the nation—North, South, East, and West. A few years ago, Texas, for example, offered very poor bass fishing; today, with over 100 large impoundments, such as the 153,000-acre Sam Rayburn and the 100,000-acre Falcon Lake on the Mexican border, Texas is one of the best bass states in the nation, rivaling even Florida.

Texas is only an example. Take a look at a new map of Alabama. Always blessed with a network of rivers like veins on a leaf, Alabama had very few lakes of any size until TVA and other organizations started building dams on the Tennessee, the Chattahoochee, the Alabama, the Black Warrior, the Coosa, the Tallapoosa, the Tombigbee, the Sipsey.

Nor are Texas and Alabama unique. Impoundments now provide excellent bass fishing in arid New Mexico and Arizona. In the Dakotas. The Carolinas. Parts of the Northeast. California. Arkansas. Even in Florida, where the largemouth has been king of freshwater for a long time, some of the hottest fishing is in impoundments.

I must point out, however, that a number of impoundments around the country are controversial. The trout angler and the salmon fisherman will surely suffer and lose wild streams, such as the Little Tennessee and the Snake in the Pacific Northwest. But the bass angler is having a heyday, and will continue to enjoy one hot spot after another.

What makes a new impoundment such a hot spot for bass? I put the question to a spokesman for TVA, and here's part of his reply:

> There are two basic reasons for rapid development of wildlife in such reservoirs. First, when a reservoir is developed, it might be described as an "ecological void." The proof of the statement "nature abhors a vacuum" is nowhere more evident than in a new reservoir.
>
> In practical terms, it means that a habitat is created without a population, and plant and animal life rush in to take advantage of this newly made haven in which there is little or no competition for space and food.
>
> Second, the appearance of wildlife in a new reservoir is the result of a temporary increase in the water's food supply. These nutrients come from the decaying of plant life native to the area before it was inundated.

As a new impoundment fills up with water, organic substances in the inundated land nurture microscopic organisms, which in turn feed larger organisms, and so on up the food chain to the bass. Indeed, there is so much food in some new impoundments that bass grow exceedingly fast. Literally. I've caught bass from the Alabama–Georgia Lake Eufaula, for example, that had grown so fast that they were out of proportion. The head was too small for the body.

Another reason for the bass bonanza is that the first-year spawn is quite successful, and more than a normal number of fry survive. When the impoundment is about two years old, it is full of yearling bass. The fishing is fantastic, with bass milling around all over the lake. Some impoundments are hot for four or five years, or even longer. But ultimately the fishing declines, at least in the number of bass caught by average anglers.

During the better years on the better lakes, almost any fairly good angler can catch a limit of bass. There's a bass at every stump, at every pocket in the shoreline, at every treetop. The bass will hit anything cast or trolled in the water. Usually, they run from 1 to 5 pounds, but of course some lunkers are caught if the original stream contained bass.

For the average angler, the bass are a good deal easier to catch in a new impoundment, not only because there are more bass to be had but also because they are all over the lake. They are comparatively easy to locate and, since they aren't yet lure shy, they are quick to bite.

I don't want to imply that all one has to do to catch a limit of bass is to get on a brand-new impoundment and start plugging away. I will say, however, that the novice has a much better chance of catching bass on a new impoundment than on an old one.

A few years after a reservoir fills up with water, the bass fishing begins to taper off. The nutrients in the new ground leach out. The lake is less

Fort Loudoun Dam in Tennessee makes a 14,600-acre impoundment. Larger impoundments cover more than 100,000 acres, and some are more than 100 miles long.

fertile than in its prime, and its biological vigor depends more and more on the richness or poorness of the watershed. Generally, shallow lakes will do better over the long run than extremely deep lakes made in gorges and canyons. This is because organic material that washes in from the watershed is more productive in shallow water than in deep.

Another reason why the bass fishing on an old impoundment is less productive for the average angler is that the bass are more difficult to locate. They have grown larger and have begun to bunch up. They have found their holding areas, often in deep water. They have selected their feeding areas and have established migration routes. Blind trolling and random casting become less and less productive. Only some 10 percent of the lake's bottom will provide likely bass habitat, and usually the figure will be a good deal less. The angler who does not know the bottom well, either from study with a depth finder or from other means, will quite likely be skunked while fishing an old impoundment, although he might pick up some small bass around the banks and at stickups.

But the fishing on some old impoundments may still be very good, at least potentially. Bass are there, and usually the fishing pressure is not too great. In old mainstream impoundments in the TVA system, for example, only about 2 percent of the bass population is caught each year. To be successful in fishing old impoundments, the bassman has to become as much hunter as fisherman. On an unfamiliar impoundment, he spends most of his time studying the bottom and hunting for bass; on an impoundment that he already knows, he spends a good part of his time riding from one spot to another, often miles apart.

Aided by all the gadgets in his bass boat, the expert will, on some days, be able to catch larger bass after the impoundment has settled down and the lunkers have holed up. On July 13, 1972, on Lake Eufaula, for example, bass pros Tom Mann and David Lockhart caught 25 bass that weighed a total of 155 pounds. The largest went over 13 pounds, and the top 17 weighed a total of 128 pounds—an average of over 7 pounds. But Lake Eufaula had passed its prime for the average angler, and there were probably a hundred bass fishermen on the lake that July 13 who caught few, if any, bass. Mann and Lockhart caught the bass because they knew where to go and what to do when they hit into a feeding spree.

Before you fish an old impoundment (or anywhere else for that matter), it pays to learn as much as you can about it. Good information can be obtained from other anglers and from tackle shops in the area, but the location of productive holes is likely to be top secret. Most anglers will tell you such things as the depth of the bass at that time of the year, the temperature of the water where the bass are holding, and so on. But they are not likely to tell you where their favorite hole is. Even if they did, you might have trouble finding it.

In some ways, fishing a natural lake is much like fishing an old impoundment. The bass are settled in their ways and will be difficult to locate. In my experience, some natural lakes are even more difficult than old impoundments. Some clear-water lakes are especially tough.

The author shows four bass taken on a small natural lake in Florida.

On the other hand, I believe that many natural lakes provide better bass fishing for the *average* angler than the old impoundments. Yet, these same lakes might provide *slower* fishing for the expert bassman. The reason for this paradox is that most natural lakes do not have as much structure or as many holding areas as an old impoundment. Having been there for thousands of years, the natural lake would have no submerged roadbeds and other man-made structure, and it would not have submerged timber. In some saucer-shaped lakes, the bass may be almost anywhere, so that depth finders and other gadgets are not as useful in pinpointing bass haunts. In this kind of situation, visible cover such as grass beds and lily pads are more important than in impoundments. Although the novice would seem to be on more equal footing with the expert in such a lake, the expert will still catch a good many more bass. He'll be quieter. He'll work his lure better. And he'll make twice as many effective casts during a day's fishing.

As a general rule, a small lake will be a good deal easier to fish than a large one. I've always felt that I can find the bass in a small lake if there are any in there. But I don't feel that way about, say, Lake Erie, which, I understand, provides some fantastic smallmouth fishing at certain times in certain places. I would not likely put a bass boat in all that water until I found out when and where. It's my opinion, then, that the average bass angler who doesn't have all the electronic gear would do better to stick to the smaller natural lakes if he has a choice.

There are well over 3 million farm ponds in this country, and some 50,000 are added each year. Oklahoma alone has more than 20,000. Although there are a few trout ponds and an increasing number of catfish ponds, most of the farm ponds are stocked with bluegills and largemouth bass.

In one sense, farm ponds are nothing but miniature impoundments. The fishing is likely to be very good for the first few years; then it starts to taper off. One big problem with the smaller farm ponds is that they become overcrowded with bluegills, which leads to a reduction in the bass spawn. And the less successful the bass spawn, the more the bluegills increase in number.

The smaller the pond, the more difficult it is to keep it in balance. If proper management techniques are followed, however, a good farm pond can provide excellent bass fishing for a number of years, or indefinitely. Even "fished out" ponds are likely to hold some large bass, but they may be difficult to catch because such a pond usually has a very crowded population of small, stunted bluegills. And most people who own the ponds don't even know the bass are there!

Since bass are bass, they will find holes and haunts in farm ponds just as they do in large impoundments. Of course, it's usually easier to find the hot spots in a farm pond than in a large impoundment simply because of the smaller area involved. Anyone who sees the terrain before a farm pond is built has an excellent opportunity to spot potential bass haunts.

I have caught a lot of bass from farm ponds, and of course I enjoyed fishing in them. Yet, somehow, I've never felt as good as when I am fishing a natural lake or a large public impoundment or a good stream. On some ponds I have felt as though I were sticking hooks into somebody's pet bass, and keeping a 3-pounder to eat would be tantamount to catching a broiler out of the owner's chicken yard!

24

Finding Hot Spots in Lakes and Impoundments

THE FIRST STEP to learning a new or otherwise unfamiliar impoundment is to obtain a topographic survey map of the area. These maps will show the contour and details of the terrain as it was before the dam was built and the reservoir filled. Symbols on the map will indicate such things as railroad tracks, roads, cemeteries, springs, streams, buildings, and man-made structures. Color coding indicates woods, marshes, scrub, orchards, and so on. And by properly reading the contour lines you can spot points, draws, knolls, and other features of the terrain. Each crook and cranny of creeks and rivers is shown.

Topographic maps can be ordered from the U.S. Geological Survey, but first get an index of maps available for each state you are interested in. (For maps west of the Mississippi River, order from Distribution Section, U.S. Geological Survey, Federal Center, Denver, Colorado 80225; for maps east of the Mississippi, order from Distribution Section, U.S. Geological Survey, 1200 Eads Street, Arlington, Virginia 22202. Standard quadrangle maps are 75 cents each.) When you are ordering maps, ask for a key to the symbols used, and be sure to ask for the pool elevation of the impoundment.

You'll need to know the pool elevation so that you can outline the impoundment on the map. Say, for example, that the pool elevation is 280 feet. Find the contour lines marked 280 and trace them with a pen or pencil. This gives you an outline of the lake.

Tracing out the impoundment is much easier if you already have a good idea of what the lake looks like. If you don't know, it helps to get a reservoir map. These are usually available from the U.S. Corps of Engineers, TVA, or agencies having cognizance over the impoundment. Sometimes they can be obtained in area sporting goods stores and bait shops. Reservoir maps are smaller than topographic maps and do not show contour lines or submerged features, but they do give you a good overall picture of the impoundment. Note also that this overall picture would be rather difficult to obtain quickly with topographic maps; set up by quadrants, topographic maps cover just so much area, so that a large impoundment may overlay a dozen maps.

After you have outlined the lake, or part of it, on a topographic map, it's easy to figure the depth at a particular contour line. If the pool elevation is 280 feet and a contour line is marked 250 feet, the depth would be 280 minus 250, or 30 feet. The problem with getting an exact depth on some impoundments is that the pool level varies from season to season, even from day to day. Even so, you can make allowances for this, and you will still have the relative depth of one area to another. For practical fishing, this relative depth is important, and exact depths can be determined by sounding or by using a good depth finder.

When your map of the impoundment is complete, study it in detail for likely bass haunts. Try to visualize what the bottom looks like. Translate all the contour lines into hills and valleys, points and draws. Some expert bassmen are constantly trying to, from a mental picture of the bottom. Bill Dance, for one, says that this helps him win bass fishing tournaments, and he thinks about bass and structure even when he is not fishing: "I find myself looking at land formations while driving along a road, and I imagine that they are underwater and how I would fish them if they were. This 'day-dreaming' has helped me many times in finding bass!"

When you are studying the map, look especially for old roadbeds, old creek channels, draws in the land, sinkholes, points, cliffs, underwater islands, flooded timber, fencerows, graveyards, buildings, and so on. In other words, determine where you want to fish before you even put the boat into the water. Next, boat to these areas with the aid of your map and pinpoint the structure with your depth finder.

It helps to find out from local anglers, or from the agency in charge of the impoundment, whether buildings and bridges and timber were left standing. In many cases, timber will be left only in certain areas. Further, it helps very much to determine from local anglers or from bait dealers and marina operators the general areas of the lake that are hot at a particular time of the year, the depth at which the bass are being caught, and similar information. Often this kind of information will eliminate at least some of the structure you have marked on your map, and more than once this kind of information has helped me catch fish when I probably wouldn't have scored on my own.

Each impoundment is different, but here are some general types of structure that often hold bass:

Points. In any lake, new or old, points often provide good bass fishing. Although these can be spotted on land and mentally projected out into the water, topographic maps show them in more detail. Note that the better fishing may be a good ways out, as shown in Figure 94. (In this figure, and in the ones that follow, an "X" indicates likely bass areas.)

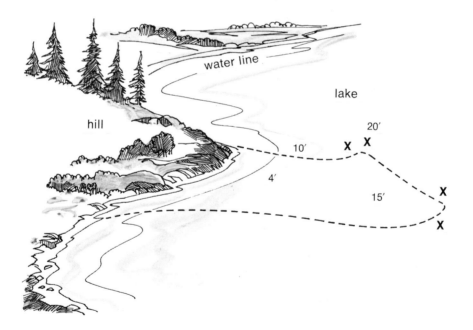

Figure 94

Draws and gulleys. These are the opposite of points, and they sometimes provide even better bass haunts. Often the bass won't be in the draws but will be near the deep water they provide. Figure 95 shows a

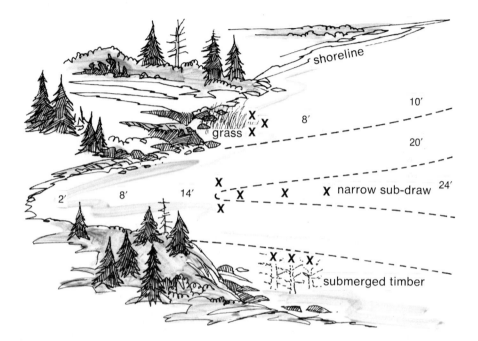

Figure 95

typical draw extending out into an impoundment from the shoreline. Pay particular attention to draws and gulleys that open into creek beds and riverbeds.

Graveyards. In impoundments old graveyards are often excellent bass holding areas. They are, of course, exhumed before the lake is flooded, and the holes are sometimes not filled.

Springs. Often springs are indicated on topographic maps, and they frequently provide an excellent, if small, bass holding area. However, they are usually difficult to locate.

Submerged farm ponds. Since topographic maps are based on aerial photographs, they will sometimes show farm ponds, and local anglers may remember the location of small farm ponds. Such ponds can provide excellent bass structure, and a typical situation is shown in Figure 96.

Submerged beaver ponds, dams, and houses can also provide good bass fishing.

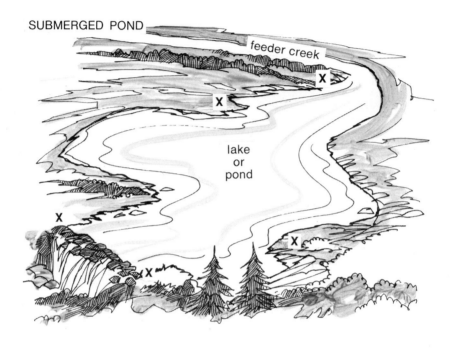

Figure 96

Old roads. Submerged roadbeds offer very good holding and feeding areas, and they are usually relatively easy to locate and follow in an impoundment. Bass will sometimes feed on the hard road surface or take cover in the ditches. A bend in the road will usually be productive, and culverts should be fished on either end. Figure 97 shows some points to fish along a typical roadbed.

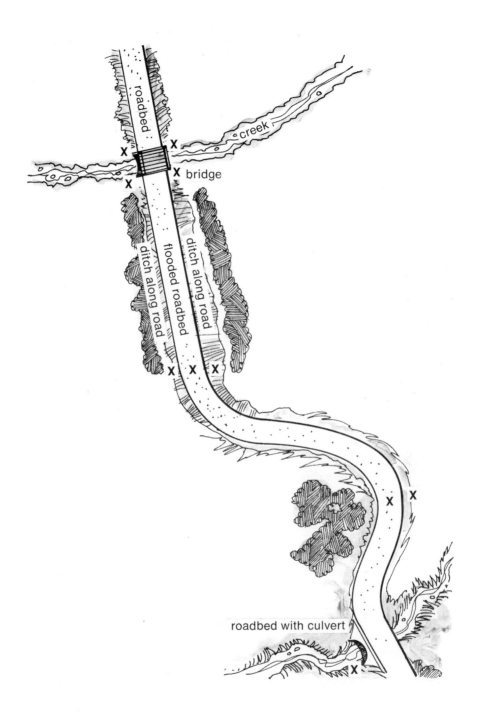

roadbed

creek

X
X
X bridge

ditch along road
flooded roadbed
ditch along road

X X X

X X

roadbed with culvert

X

Figure 97

Creeks. Submerged creek beds are generally the most reliable types of structure in impoundments. By running the boat in a zigzag pattern, you will locate the creek bed relatively easily and be able to follow it with a depth finder. Figure 98 shows a typical submerged creek and some likely spots for bass. A horseshoe bend is generally one of the better spots if the depth is right. Note that the outside part of a bend is usually better than the inside.

In addition to providing structure and substructure, as well as probable migration routes from holding areas to feeding areas, the creek beds will, in some impoundments, have a slow current during drawdown periods. This current can be conducive to good bass fishing. Bass fishing in Florida's Lake Talquin, for instance, is much better during drawdown periods, at which time the creek beds and the riverbed are the most likely spots for large bass.

Rocks. Any kind of rock structure, whether it be a rocky ledge, a large boulder, or simply a rocky bottom, can provide excellent bass habitat and feeding areas. Smallmouth and spotted bass are especially fond of rocky bottom and rocky inclines.

Timber. Submerged timber can provide very good bass fishing, especially for largemouth bass. Where lots of timber is left standing in an impound-ment, however, it's best to look for some substructure or some break in the structure. A knoll in timber may be excellent, and timber lines along open fields are sometimes good.

After you have located some likely spots and your topographic map contains a few dozen X's, your next step is to find them in the water. This is not easy. A knack for practical navigation helps, and skill and experience at using a depth finder also help. The angler with his first depth finder is unsure of what all those red flashes really indicate, but before long he is able to locate potential hot spots without wasting too much time. It's best to start out with a small section of your map, preferably at creek beds or roadbeds because they are easy to spot and follow out with the depth finder.

When you do find a spot, fish it for about thirty minutes. Make sure that your lure gets deep enough and into the structure, using the tech-niques discussed in Chapters 14 and 15. If you don't catch any bass after thirty minutes, move on. But before you go, mark the hole well by tri-angulation so that it will be easier to find in case you want to fish it at a different time of day or during a different season of the year.

Triangulation is a visual method of pinpointing your position on a body of water. The trick is to align two sets of landmarks so that connecting

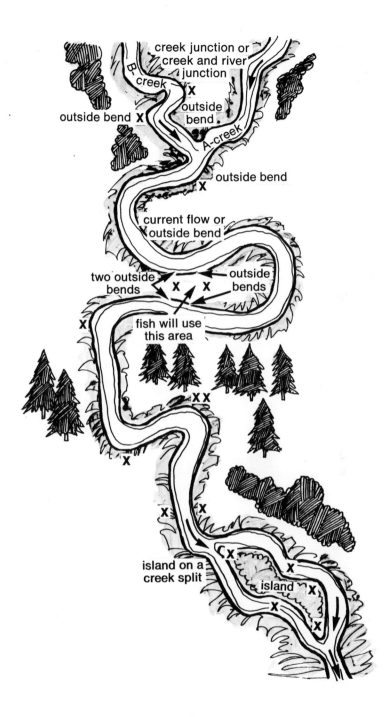

Figure 98

lines, if projected, would intersect at the spot you occupy. For example, you have found a hole well out in an impoundment. The first step in the triangulation process is to line up two landmarks and point the bow of the boat directly toward them. Then find two more aligned landmarks on either side of the boat. Figure 99 shows a typical example.

Be sure to indicate the landmarks on your map or in a notebook. Also indicate the approximate distance from the hole to the shore. If you plan to fish the impoundment often, it's a good idea to jot down a description of the hole and give it a name.

Although triangulation sounds easy on paper, it can sometimes be difficult in actual fishing conditions. It can, in fact, be almost impossible on large lakes in flat country. One trick is to mark the spot temporarily with a buoy marker and then move the boat around the area until you can

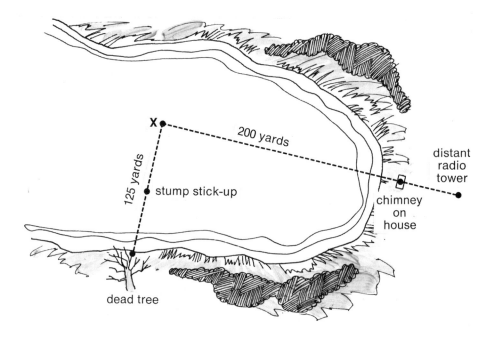

Figure 99

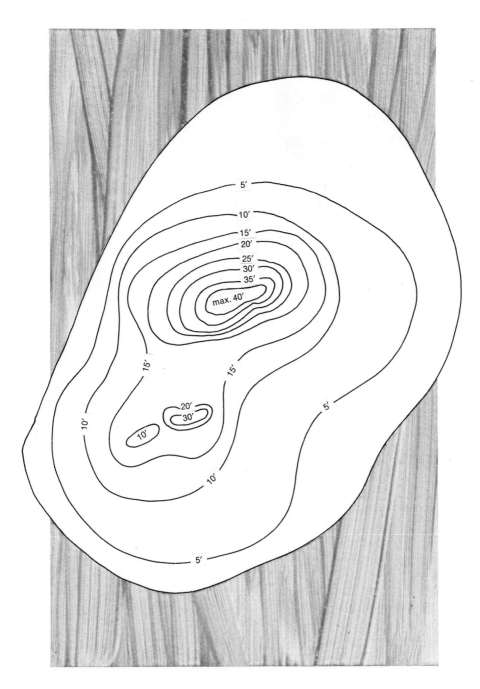

Figure 100

successfully triangulate a spot. Next, determine the distance and the direction to your fishing hole. Note the compass heading or line up the buoy marker with a particular point on the land. Record all the data and retrieve your buoy marker. When you want to find the hole again, find the triangulated spot and then proceed to the fishing hole.

A good piece of structure will produce fish year after year, although there may be a good deal of seasonal variation. For this reason, it's best to note the time of the year, the depth, and the water temperature along with the triangulation data. This information may be of value the following year.

Even if you don't plan to fish the impoundment again, it pays to obtain depth and temperature data from a productive spot. It could be that you have found a pattern, and this information will permit you to locate similar structure at the same depth in other parts of the impoundment. Most expert bassmen put a lot of stock in pattern fishing these days, and it makes sense.

One reason that natural lakes are tough to fish, even with modern electronic aids, is that topographic maps do not show contour lines and structure for them, simply because these features would not be evident on aerial photographs. If a natural lake does have deep holes and some sort of structure—such as spring holes, submerged islands, or underwater cliffs—the bassman will surely profit by finding them. But it is more difficult without the aid of topographic maps.

Some states do publish hydrological maps, and they may be available through the Fish and Game Commission (or whatever it's called in a particular state). Hydrological maps show the general depth of the lake with contour lines, but the maps are not nearly as detailed as topographic maps. Even so, the contour lines alone will sometimes indicate likely spots for bass. Look for places where the lines tend to converge. Figure 100 shows what a hydrological map might look like for a small lake.

One key to fishing a natural lake without the aid of a hydrological map is to take a close look at the surrounding terrain. A bluff on one side of the lake may indicate deep water, and a flat area is likely to extend on out into the water. A point, or a draw, will also tend to jut on out into the lake.

The persistent angler can of course learn the bottom of a natural lake quite well without any electronic equipment. But it's usually a long, slow process. It can be accelerated sharply with the aid of a good depth finder. I learned more about Lake Weir in two days with a depth finder than I did in two years without one!

25

Chasing the Schools

ALTHOUGH THE LARGER BASS do tend to bunch up in good deep holes and can accurately be called gregarious, they are not really school fish in the sense that mullet and shad and mackerel are. They act as individuals rather than as a group, and they don't gather and move about in vast hordes. When small bass do seem to be schooling by the hundreds—and I've seen them frothing the water by the acre—they are actually feeding on schooling forage fish, such as shad. I have stood on bluffs overlooking clear-water impoundments and watched great schools of shad lie suspended like underwater clouds. Millions of shad. When bass start tearing into such a school, the action can be fast and furious.

More often than not, schooling bass will be small—from 1 to 2 pounds, or often smaller. But larger bass do feed on shad, and sometimes they will be under the smaller bass that thrash about on the surface. One theory is that the small bass kill or maim lots of bait fish, and the larger, lazier bass grab these as they flutter down. In this case, letting the lure sink would be the best way to catch the larger bass.

I've read that schooling bass will hit anything, but this definitely hasn't been the case in my experience. Fishing for schooling bass can be frustrating. Sometimes they won't hit what you're throwing them. I've seen

Stringers like this, taken from Toledo Bend on the Texas–Louisiana border in July 1973, are not uncommon if the angler knows how to spot and fish the schools.

anglers cast into schools and chase them around for an hour without a strike. Yet, the bass seemed so thick that the odds would seem to favor foul-hooking one or two. Usually, the trouble is that the angler is not fishing with anything that looks like a shad, or isn't getting the right action, or doesn't have the right-sized lure. I would advise anyone who plans to fish for schooling bass to stock up with several sizes of lures that look like shad or that behave like shad in the water.

The shad-colored stick lures can be jerked about on top, preferably in a zigzag pattern. Sometimes the Rapalas and ThinFin lures can be effective if they are jerked about on top, but these are not ideal because the smaller sizes are light and difficult to cast. Probably the most effective lures for schooling bass are the small, heavy lead baits. The tail spinners (described in Chapters 12 and 13) are good when fished fast to attract bass thrashing about on the surface, or sometimes when allowed to sink 5 or 10 feet and then retrieved fast. Be sure to keep a tight line while the lure is sinking, in case a bass mistakes it for an injured shad.

One big advantage of the small lead lures is that they can be cast for long distances, even into wind. And distance can be quite important, too, when you're fishing for schooling bass. The farther you keep the boat from the school, the less likely you are to spook them. And, in many cases, the long cast allows the angler to get in a quick cast or two before the school sounds.

Bass school to one degree or another on many large lakes and impoundments in the South and Southwest. They will also school on more northern impoundments, but not as often. They sometimes school in small lakes and even in rivers, but usually the best schooling action will be in large impoundments during the warmer months of the year. Typically, schooling action will be heavier on calm days between midmorning and midafternoon.

Anyone interested in fishing for schooling bass should always keep an eye peeled for them. Sea gulls swarming around and diving down often indicate that bass are knocking shad around on the surface, so that schooling activity can at times be spotted from some distance away. And of course the bass and the shad cause a ruckus. On some large lakes and impoundments, it sometimes pays to run the boat around looking for schooling activity. This is called jump fishing. I have not fished in this manner myself, but here's a report from Al Eason, a professional guide in Texas, as published in the 1973 *Garcia Fishing Annual*:

Schooling bass were a different matter. They were constantly on the move, gorging themselves on the restless schools of silvery shad. To take them, Toledo fishermen devised one of the wildest, most exciting methods known to bass fishermen. With schooling bass, a fast fishing rig was a must.

This writer uses a 70-horse Chrysler engine, and most of the other Toledo guides use propulsion units of equal, or more, horsepower. These large engines are necessary on such a large lake and their added power and speed proved excellent for chasing after school bass. The fish were on top for only a minute or so at most, and seconds were often the difference between success and failure.

So critical was this time factor that lines were tied directly to the lure without the usual snap-swivel. This gimmick allowed the lure to be reeled snug against the tiptop of the rod, where it jutted out at an angle, a position where it was impossible for the lure's hooks to foul the line. Passengers in the boat carried their rods at ready, while the operator placed his rod in a position where it could be reached the moment the boat stopped.

Schools of surfacing bass were located by sight and sound. While waiting for a school to break, the boat was turned toward the darker portion of the lake, where light reflection made it easier to spot the first skittering shad. The instant active fish were heard or sighted, the engine was cranked, and the throttle slammed wide open. As the racing boat came within casting range of the school, a quick twist of the wheel brought the boat broadside to the school and the engine was shut off. If the school was reached in time, three instant hook-ups often resulted from the first casts.

When the schools were active, three casts per man were par for any one school. To waste more time than this on a school which sounded was to miss more probable action on other fish in the area which were active. Fishing the school bass was as thrilling as a boat race, as wild as water rodeo, and as productive as a fisherman's day dream. Limit catches were often taken before noon.

As I said, I've never deliberately set out to hunt for schooling bass. But if I did, I would surely want a fast boat, as Al Eason suggested. I would also want a good pair of binoculars and a pair of polarized sunglasses with flip-up lenses. For fishing gear, I would want a good open-faced spinning reel with a 5-to-1 retrieve ratio, and I would have it spooled with 10-pound monofilament. I would want a 7-foot rod of medium action, and I would want a bunch of small, heavy lures. In short, I would be rigged for distance casting.

26

Fishing Rivers and Streams

SMALL OF THE MOST ENJOYABLE bass fishing I've ever done was on float trips down rivers and streams. As a rule, however, rivers and streams are not as productive as lakes and impoundments, and especially not for trophy bass.

Moreover, floating down a stream isn't really the best way to fish it, although it is certainly the most convenient and the most popular way. Although a lot of bass have been caught on float trips—and some streams, such as the White River in the Ozarks, are noted for this sport—it is better, if feasible, to proceed upstream instead of floating downstream. The reason is that bass invariably face upstream while waiting for food to come by. Assuming that you cast ahead of the boat, an upstream approach permits you to retrieve your lure with the current, so that bass will be more likely to see it approach; if, on the other hand, you are floating downstream and retrieving the lure against the current, the bass would not see the lure until it passed them. Most bass anglers don't like to retrieve a lure with the current, but that's the way it should be done.

The best bet, then, is to proceed upstream by motor, then stop the boat just below choice holes. The boat can be anchored, beached, or secured to an overhanging tree limb. Brush hooks often come in handy on some streams. Stopping the boat permits you to fish the hole thoroughly instead of merely getting in a few quick casts while drifting by. Although you don't cover as much of the stream as when you are floating, the upstream approach is usually more productive, and you can usually get in just as many *effective* casts in a given time period. The reason is that most of the larger bass in a stream will be in or near deep holes. Thus, many casts on a typical float trip are quite wasted.

Another good argument for the upstream approach is that the bass are not as likely to see you coming. Remember that bass will more often than not be facing upstream, and they don't have eyes in the rear. Also, boat noises carry much farther downstream than upstream.

For fishing small streams, a canoe or a 12-foot aluminum johnboat is better than a superduper bass boat. During the past few years, Old Town and other companies have started making light one-man canoes. Sportspal makes a very light (29½-pound) two-man canoe that can be lifted over logs or portaged around waterfalls, and Orvis is marketing an 11-foot cedar canoe that weighs under 25 pounds! But the best way to fish a stream, or at least some streams, is to wade.

I prefer a bait-casting outfit for fishing streams. They are more accurate than spinning or spincast outfits, as explained in Chapter 2. And accuracy in casting is often more important on streams than in impoundments and lakes; stream bass like to lie on the shady side of stumps and logs and are fond of getting under low, overhanging brush. A spinning outfit, on the other hand, does come in handy for light lures, and a fly rod will sometimes catch more bass than either casting or spinning gear. But if I could take only one rig, it would surely be a casting outfit.

Although top-water plugs will catch stream bass, they are usually not as productive as underwater baits. Top-water plugs are more effective when allowed to drift downstream with the current, but they should be twitched from time to time. One big problem with fishing top-water lures in streams is that if you do let them float downstream, you'll too often have too much slack line when the bass hits and therefore won't be able to set the hook properly.

Swimming plugs, such as Creek Chub's old reliable Pikie, will catch river bass, and a deep diver like the Hellbender is often ideal for streams with sloping banks. Plastic worms and pork eels are very effective, and I like to cast them out and let them drift down, sinking slowly, with the current; I usually avoid those heavy slip sinkers, but I do sometimes use a weighted hook. Spinner baits are also very effective in some streams, especially those with clear water. I use both in-line spinners and safety-pin designs. I like to use spinners in deep holes, and I sometimes prefer to fish them downstream instead of upstream. The trick here is to make a long cast and keep a tight line while the lure is going down. The tight line and the current will keep the spinner working, and most of the strikes will come while the lure is sinking. When casting a spinner into the current, I retrieve it just fast enough to keep the blade turning.

Stretches of streams immediately below dams often provide excellent fishing. Called tail waters, these streams are likely to have cool, well-oxygenated water. Usually, the small, heavy lures—such as jigs—work better in tail waters because the current is so swift. Owing to this swift and often erratically turbulent water, fishing in tail waters can be dangerous, and I, for one, have learned from several close calls to keep boats well below the dams.

Another productive spot in some streams is in much more placid water where the river spreads out into a large pool. Some pools of this kind are so large that they are called lakes, and these are often excellent spots for the largemouth bass. In fact, the world's record largemouth was caught from such a spot, called Lake Montgomery, in Georgia's Ocmulgee River. A sort of wide horseshoe bend in the river, Lake Montgomery has now pretty much filled in with sand, so it is shallow and weedy.

Although dams, pollution, and channelization have taken their toll, there are thousands of excellent bass streams in this country, and most of them are not heavily fished. Moreover, stream fishing is good almost any day of the year! Stream bass are not as sensitive as lake bass to changes in the weather. For one thing, the temperature in a stream is usually pretty much the same from one spot to another because of the current. And wind that would blow an angler off a large impoundment or large lake is often of no consequence on a stream.

For example, one January I attended an outdoor writers' meeting in Tallahassee, Florida. I can't speak for the other scribes, but I for one had high hopes of tangling into one of those 14-pound largemouths that have made Lake Jackson famous. We were, we thought, all lined up with guides, boats, and so on. Well, it froze. It was the coldest I've ever known it in Florida, and the wind was awfully high. The guides didn't think we were going to catch any fish, and the night before, they seemed reluctant even to think about getting up in that freezing weather at daylight. But, yes, they wanted us to fish. The drift of their thinking was that we should get an early start and be on the lake by ten o'clock!

I happened to meet a couple of local anglers, and they suggested that I join them on a little river—the Wacissa—southeast of Tallahassee. It turned out to be one of the most beautiful little streams I've ever seen and was completely primitive. We caught some bass and cooked them for lunch on the riverbank. It was a great trip. In this case, fishing a stream saved the day, at least for me.

In ordinary weather, however, an expert could catch more bass from Lake Jackson and nearby Lake Talquin than on the Wacissa. This is largemouth country, and largemouths tend to prefer lakes to streams. I don't mean that there aren't good largemouth streams. There are. Some of the best are the small brackish-water rivers on the Atlantic and Gulf Coasts, and these streams are generally neglected by bass fishermen. Anyone plugging these streams might tie into a snook or a tarpon, in addition to the largemouth! By the way, brackish-water bass usually hit better on a rising tide, and bass in almost all streams hit better when the river is rising slightly.

The smallmouth bass and the spotted bass prefer suitable streams to lakes, although the world's record smallmouth and the world's record spotted bass were caught in impoundments. A good smallmouth stream has a gradient of no less than 5 feet per mile and no more than 25 feet per mile. Also, the smallmouth will spawn only over fine gravel, and at temperatures between 60 and 70 degrees F.

Before you fish any stream, it's best to find out what sort of bass grow in it. This information should influence your choice of lure (smallmouth and spotted bass prefer smaller lures than a largemouth) and to an extent where you fish on the stream. In a good smallmouth stream, you should concentrate on the end of riffles and the swift water at the head of large pools. In a largemouth stream, concentrate on the slower-moving water in the large pools. On some Florida streams, such as the St. Johns, consider using very large lures, such as the 7-inch Rapalas and 12-inch plastic worms, because this is trophy largemouth country and you are more likely to interest a 17-pounder with a large bait.

27

Fishing by Sun and Moon

In most impoundments and in some natural lakes, the larger bass establish a daily pattern. There may be any number of seasonal variations and local nuances, and sometimes abrupt changes owing perhaps to such physical conditions as the water's dissolved oxygen content, but by and large the daily pattern involves deep water, shallow water, and structure routes from one to the other.

Let's start at noonday. The larger bass are probably deep, preferably in a hole that has protective structure or cover. They may mill about a bit and will feed on anything that happens past, but generally they stay put. At some point in the afternoon, they start migrating to feeding areas. If possible, they will move from deep water to shallow along some route that provides cover and shade. They'll follow the same route during their morning migration from shallow water to the deep midday haunts.

The daily pattern may vary somewhat with the seasons and with geographic location. During cold weather, the bass tend to stay in the deeper holes; winter slows them down, and they are less inclined to forage about simply because they don't require as much food. But on warm, sunny days following extended cold spells, the bass may move into shallow water.

During summer, the bass are likely to stay in deep holes during most of the day, moving out only very late in the afternoon or at night. Summer is, however, the time to fish for schooling bass, as discussed in Chapter 25.

During fall, the bass start their movement toward shallow feeding grounds earlier in the day, and they may generally spend more time in shallow water. Bass sometimes go on a feeding binge in the fall, thereby providing some excellent fishing along banks and visible cover.

During spring, some of the bass will be on the bed or else looking for bedding spots in shallow water. They'll be there all day. Others will still be in deeper water, and still others will be at intermediate depths. In short, bass, like young men, have the urge to roam about in spring. Bass spawn as early as February (or even January) here in Florida and as late as mid-summer in northern states. But, generally, spring is spawning time and is traditionally the favorite time to fish for bass. I dare say that anglers who don't own depth finders and other expensive electronic aids to deep-water fishing catch more lunker bass in spring than in all other seasons combined.

Bedding bass are comparatively easy to locate. Their shallow white beds —fanned out to 3 or 4 feet in diameter—are easy to see in all but the murkiest waters. In addition to being easy to spot, spawning bass are usually easy to catch. Because of a territorial imperative and an instinct to protect their eggs, bass will attack anything that moves into the bed. They bite a lure not so much because they are fooled into thinking it is fit to eat but because they are angry and protective of their young.

In some states, game laws protect bass during spawning season, but many states have no such laws. Studies made some time ago on TVA impoundments helped determine that angling pressure, even during spawning season, had no appreciable effect on bass populations. But these studies were made before anglers started using scientific instruments to help find bass in deep water. On a year-round basis, very few fish were caught then as compared to what modern anglers can do today. Although the black bass is in no danger, and new impoundments increase its habitat each year, I believe that some lakes would provide better bass fishing throughout the year if the spawning season were closed either annually or biannually.

Most bass anglers who fish at night do so during the warmer months, but they may be missing some good fishing on chilly nights. In fact, the world's-record spotted bass was caught from North Alabama's Lake Lewis Smith at night in February!

Generally, night fishing for bass compares quite favorably with daylight fishing, especially on lakes where pleasure-boat traffic is heavy and water skiers make sport of buzzing anglers. But novice bass anglers who have been led to believe that they can fill the boat merely by getting on the lake after dark and casting away at random are likely to be disappointed. Night fishing is different, and it isn't for everybody.

Bass prefer certain places by night as well as by day, so that pinpoint casting into cover or structure is important—and it's a good deal more difficult at night. An angler must have a finely honed feeling for his tackle, and his timing must often be based on senses other than plain vision. In other words, he must cast accurately even when he can't see clearly. Thorough familiarity with his gear helps, and so does thorough familiarity with the waters he plans to fish.

Here are some other considerations:

Equipment. A good bait-casting outfit spooled with a braided line is my choice for night fishing. Monofilament line, on any kind of reel, causes too many problems, and line twist is common at night because of fouled lures. A bait-casting reel with a large power handle works better at night than one with a regular handle.

Lights. Strong lights attract crappie and some other fish, but they send bass to cover—fast. Consequently, flashlights and boat spots should be used sparingly. When changing lures or inspecting tackle, I normally use a battery-powered fluorescent lamp placed on the boat's deck so that it won't shine directly into the water. If I'm fishing alone on a dark night, I like to have a frogging-type headlight just in case I tie into a lunker and need both hands free while boating it.

Choice of lure. I would say that most night anglers use Jitterbugs and similar surface lures. They catch bass—lots of them at times. But I think that more night fishermen ought to try spoons, plastic worms, and other weedless lures. Black is the traditional color for night fishing, but it's worthwhile to try other colors too. On one of the most successful fishing trips I ever had, I used Johnson Silver Minnows and white pork rind on a moonlit night.

I prefer a lure that I don't have to see to tell whether or not it's running true. These lures include the safety-pin spinner baits with large blades, sonic lures that impart a discernible vibration, and surface lures that make a distinct sound, such as the Jitterbug and the Sputterbug.

Safety. Never run a boat fast at night, and certainly not in unfamiliar waters. It's best to wear a life jacket at all times, especially when you are fishing alone. Tell somebody where you plan to fish and when you'll be back. On large lakes, take a compass and know how to use it. Remember that things look different at night, and mishaps are more likely to occur than in the day.

Insect repellent. Don't forget to take along some sort of insect repellent when you are fishing at night during the warmer months. But keep it off your lures.

Fishing columns in many newspapers, as well as in some of the outdoor magazines, publish daily, weekly, or monthly Solunar Tables. Worked out over three decades ago by John Alden Knight, the tables are based on the changing position of the sun and moon in relation to the earth.

The Solunar Tables show the time of day when feeding activity is likely to be at its peak. Each daily listing includes a major and a minor period for a particular longitude, and the periods for the immediate future can be calculated by adding about fifty minutes per day. If, for example, a minor period is listed for 1:00 P.M. on Monday, the minor will be at 1:50 P.M. on Tuesday and at 2:40 P.M. on Wednesday. A major period lasts from two to three and a half hours; a minor, from three-quarters hour to one and a half hours. Although the minor is shorter, bass may sometimes feed more actively than during the major.

Some anglers fish religiously by the major and minor periods, but I personally don't put that much faith in them. I've caught too many lunker bass at times when neither the major nor the minor periods were in effect, and I've too often been skunked during major and minor periods. I do, however, believe that anglers have a better chance of catching bass during a major or minor. But I don't think they should stay off the lake merely because a major or minor isn't in effect. I'm certain that those people who swear by the tables will indeed catch more bass during a major or minor, but I suggest that they probably fish harder and with more confidence during those periods. It is, in my opinion, an error for the bassman to explain success or failure by whether or not the fish are biting. The better philosophy is that the bass will bite at any time of the day or night if the angler can locate them and present the right lure in the right way.

There is no doubt something to the tables, and many anglers can plan their fishing trips accordingly. Believers with enough leisure to choose when they fish should purchase a copy of *Moon Up—Moon Down*, by John Alden Knight. First published in 1942, this 163-page book has recently been reprinted in limited edition. And the real Solunar enthusiast might want to purchase a Solunagraph wristwatch, available for a mere $195 from Orvis.

Apart from the Solunar tables, some anglers fish by the phases of the moon or by "signs" on calendars and almanacs. Many say, for example, that fishing is best three days before and three days after a full moon. I don't say that these people are loony, but again I don't believe a man ought to stay at home because the moon is full or isn't full.

In addition to times of day, seasonal variations, and the phases of the moon, here are some physical variables that have an effect on bass fishing:

Temperature. A few years ago, the top outdoor writers expounded a belief that temperature was the key to locating and catching bass. Supposedly, largemouth bass were more comfortable in temperatures from 65 to 75 degrees F.; smallmouth and spotted bass, from 60 to 70 degrees F. The temperature theory has not been disproved and is not widely held in disfavor, but recent studies tend to indicate that bass, within reason, don't give a damn about the temperature (and I've caught bass at temperatures from 40 to 85 degrees F.), that they don't seek out the ideal temperature range, and that they will freely move through a rather large thermal gradient. Consider, for example, a study conducted by a TVA biologist at Muscle Shoals, Alabama, near a steam-plant discharge.

Miniature sensors were implanted in bass before they were released near the discharge. In August 1972 a largemouth bass moved through water from 80 to 93.5 degrees F. during a period of thirty-three hours; a smallmouth, from 73.6 to 90.5 degrees F. in eleven hours; another smallmouth, from 46 to 63.3 degrees F. in eighty-three hours. Other specimens also traversed similar thermal gradients. This study was not by any means conclusive, and the data probably haven't been fully analyzed at the time of this writing, but the biologist in charge of the research told me that the best conclusion he could draw under the circumstances is that bass are not repelled by rather steep thermal gradients and that they will voluntarily cross them.

Yet, temperature should not by any means be disregarded. As explained in Chapter 4, temperature affects a bass's metabolic rate, which in turn affects how actively a bass feeds and how much it eats. In short, it still pays the angler to seek out bass within the ideal temperature range. They'll be more likely to hit a lure and will move farther and faster for it. If the angler is fishing in temperatures below the ideal range, then smaller lures and slower retrieves are in order.

Light intensity. The importance of light intensity was discussed along with light meters in Chapter 4, and in connection with lure color in Chapter 10. As was pointed out, bass have fixed pupils and no eyelids. The only way they can control the amount of light that reaches the retina is to seek out shade or go deeper where the sunlight doesn't penetrate as intensely. It is now believed that bass, especially larger ones, are uncomfortable in bright sunlight, although they will at times feed in it and will of course bed in it.

Whether or not large bass really are physically uncomfortable in bright light may be open to question, especially in view of the fact that the smaller bass are often in bright light. But, for whatever reason, larger bass do avoid bright light most of the time. Here's John Weiss's summary ("The

Best Bass Fishing Starts Where Light Stops," May 1973 *Sports Afield*) of some recent experiments on the effect of light intensity on bass:

By conducting a number of experiments on Lake Mead in Nevada, one group of fishery biologists confirmed that bass will go to almost any length to avoid bright light. To the uninitiated, this body of water is gin clear, very deep, and relatively cover-free. During the course of their experimentation, divers donned scuba gear and took bright flood-light underwater in search of big bass. They found them.

Previous studies, by the way, have shown that fish seldom fear skin divers, for some unknown reason. Divers can often closely approach large game fish underwater and sometimes even touch them without the fish registering alarm. They seem to just slowly mosey along, continuing about their normal activity. Poke a finger at them and they may quickly dart a few feet away, only to swing about, out of curiosity I suppose, and return to the immediate vicinity.

Upon first seeing the biologist's bright floodlights, however, most of the bass started making a beeline for much deeper water in search of protective darkness. The divers pursued them with the lights turned on full blast and most of the bass retreated so deep, they entered the oxygen-void hypolimnion.

Follow-up studies related by the legendary Buck Perry, a physics professor from North Carolina State who somehow got side-tracked and is now considered one of the country's foremost bass experts, were conducted on a crystal-clear southern impoundment. Here, as before, the bass responded in a similar manner when biologists lowered bright lights into the depths, the illumination forcing the fish to unbelievable extremes.

To further dispute long-held fishing beliefs, fishery biologists are likewise starting to admit that, perhaps, water temperature may not have the great influence upon bass that we have been led to believe. At least, not as great an influence as bright light.

Bass, like all fish, are cold-blooded creatures. This means their bodies are always the same temperature as the water they're living in, so they are comfortable at most any temperature. While a bass is just as comfortable in 55 degree water as he is in 75 degree water, however, it is his metabolic rate and consequent behavior that is influenced by certain temperatures. This means that each species has a certain temperature range in which they can be expected to exhibit *maximum activity*. Below the preferred temperature, their metabolism is slowed considerably, and they require less fuel to sustain their systems. Above the preferred range, they become sluggish.

While a bass's spawning urge and desire to feed, no doubt, is primarily regulated by changes in water temperature, these fish are still

highly adaptable creatures. They can and do tolerate water-tempera-
ture extremes, and it has been found that they will venture into less-
favorable water temperatures to avoid bright light. So anglers should
consequently take into consideration light penetration of water first,
and water temperature second, not vice versa as has been customary.

Under normal conditions in which bass are not being pursued by the
bright lights of biologists, there is really only one thing that will limit
the depth at which a bass will go to avoid bright light—the presence of
summer stratification in which a thermocline forms, separating the
lower, oxygen-void layer of water from the upper, oxygen-saturated
layer.

Mr. Weiss's comments about water temperature support what I said
earlier in this chapter, but his comments about the summer stratification
may need updating in view of more recent experience. The importance of
oxygen content, and the extent to which it can vary independently of
temperature will be discussed later. Meanwhile, back to light penetration.

One reason that shallow-water fishing is better early and late in the
day is because most of the sunlight is reflected from the water when it hits
at an angle of 30 degrees or less. But, after midmorning, underwater
illumination increases to a maximum at noonday; then it begins to taper
off again.

Underwater illumination is also caused by diffused "sky light," but this
is almost negligible as compared to direct sunlight. Consequently midmorning to midafternoon fishing in shallow water is better on overcast days
than on bright days. In fact, some of the best daylong shallow-water fishing I've ever had was during a slow drizzle.

Wind ripples and heavier wave action also have an effect on underwater
illumination. From midmorning to midafternoon, waves tend to divert
some of the sunlight from direct penetration. Early and late in the day,
however, wave action will catch some of the light rays and cause more underwater illumination than would occur with a glass-smooth surface!

An obvious factor in underwater illumination is how murky the water is.
Although I believe that it's usually much more difficult to catch bass in clear
water, I'm not entirely convinced that absolute light intensity has too much
to do with it. I think it's entirely possible that bass in a clear-water lake are
accustomed to a greater light intensity than bass in a murky lake. In other
words, the ideal "comfort luminosity," if that's the term, is not an absolute
quantity but is relative, and varies from one lake to another.

In any case, the new emphasis on the importance of light penetration
bears out what savvy bass anglers have known for some time now. It's best
to fish deep (or under heavy cover) when the sun is high and bright,

especially in summer when the sun is directly overhead and penetration is at a maximum. Similarly, you should fish more shallow as light penetration falls off, either because of the angle of the sun or because of cloud cover.

Generally, a lot of small bass will be in shallow water regardless of light intensity, and most of the real lunker bass will be either in the deeper water or under heavy cover. And, of course, regardless of light intensity schooling bass are often caught near the top.

Barometric pressure. Some bass anglers keep an eye on the barometer, and atmospheric pressure does apparently have an effect on bass. Some anglers believe that bass feed better when the barometer is rather high, less when it is low; others believe that it doesn't matter whether the barometer is high or low, so long as it is steady. But whether the pressure is rising or falling may be the more important factor. Bass usually feed more on a rising barometer, so that excellent fishing can be had when the pressure is low and rising. On the other hand, bass can feed furiously when the barometer starts to drop quickly immediately before a storm. I know of some out-of-state anglers who hightail it to Florida's Orange Lake whenever a hurricane is brewing, and they have made some astounding catches.

I don't think that anyone knows exactly why or how barometric pressure affects a bass's feeding activity. One theory, however, is that low pressure together with a warming trend causes insect pupae to burst. The hatch attracts panfish into shallow water, and the panfish attract bass. When high pressure returns, the hatch stops and the fish go back to deeper water to feed on crustaceans. If this theory is correct, an angler should fish shallow in low pressure and deep during high pressure. But of course other factors must also be considered. In any case, I have no control of the barometric pressure, so I usually ignore it and fish whenever I can.

Dissolved-oxygen content. Although "oxygen-structure fishing" is the latest development in bassing techniques, the importance of dissolved oxygen to healthy fish populations has been known for some time. Over three decades ago, the U.S. Bureau of Fisheries conducted studies that resulted in a designation of parts per million (PPM) for measuring dissolved-oxygen content. Water can hold amounts of oxygen from zero to 20 PPM, and this range was divided into four sections: 0 to 3 PPM, 3 to 5 PPM, 5 to 13 PPM, and 13 to 20 PPM.

The lower range, 0 to 3 PPM, will not sustain fish. Water containing 3 to 5 PPM will support bass only for brief periods; within a few minutes, they become sluggish, and they will more than likely die within three days. At the high end of the scale, water containing 13 to 20 PPM is not desirable; fish in such supersaturated water are susceptible to oxygen poisoning, which can cause sudden death much like a stroke.

The fishing action, then, is in the middle range, from 5 to 13 PPM. Called the comfort zone, it is the range in which bass are likely to feed or hit artificial lures. As Byron Dalrymple said in his article "How to Find and Catch Trophy Bass" (*Field & Stream*, January 1972):

> . . . Plentiful oxygen equals supreme comfort and well-being for any bass, but especially for the large old bigmouth.
>
> This is one reason why winter months in the South are best. The lower the temperature, up to a point, the more dissolved oxygen available. Water in the mid-60's supports several parts per million more than at summer highs up toward the 80's. In addition, oxygen content has greater stability in winter when plant photosynthesis and decomposition are both at a low ebb. In those deep, cool, only mildly fertile lakes perfect for growing trophy bass, oxygen content changes little. In weedy, fertile lakes, drastic ups and downs occur. In any lake containing green aquatic plants, large bass will be most active beginning in late afternoon, for oxygen content is highest then. This is especially true in quiet bays and arms where wind action is minimal. The time of the least dissolved oxygen is dawn, because photosynthesis has been dormant during the night.

At the time Dalrymple wrote his article, the ordinary bass angler had no convenient way to measure oxygen content. Apparently scientific monitoring devices were available, but few bass anglers knew about them, where to obtain them, and how to use them. It was only in 1973 that dissolved-oxygen content came to the forefront of bass fishing, primarily because of the advertising and publicity drive launched by Bass-Ox, Inc., developers of the Sentry oxygen monitor.

Before then, most bass fishermen were concerned only (if at all) about a layer of water below the thermocline. In the warmer months, the water in lakes can stratify into thermal layers. The upper, warm-water layer is called the epilimnion, and the lower, cold-water layer is called the hypolimnion. An in-between layer, of variable depth, is called a thermocline. Below the thermocline, the oxygen content may drop too low to sustain bass.

Until quite recently, the thermocline was usually located by lowering a temperature sensor into the water and noting the depth at which the temperature dropped fast. But it's now realized that a lake can have drastic changes in dissolved-oxygen content *independently* of temperature. As explained in the November/December 1973 *BASSmaster* magazine:

> Better than 94 percent of the oxygen in the water comes from microscopic oxygen generating systems such as phytoplankton, photosyn-

thetic bacteria, and photosynthetic algae. About five percent of the
dissolved oxygen comes from the visible plants, such as moss, grass,
lily pads, etc. These only create oxygen during the daylight hours. But,
these same plants use oxygen during the night in their growth processes
and actually may use more oxygen than they produce during the day.
Therefore, a weed bed, moss field, etc., with a high PPM reading late
in the afternoon may be oxygen poor the next morning. The other one
percent or so of oxygen is taken from the air through wave action and
rain, which is mostly anoxic, and only creates dissolved oxygen through
its bouncing-aeration action. Also, incoming streams, visible or underground, may have become oxygenated by recent rains. Normally
though, underground streams and springs are anoxic.

The same organisms that produce 94 percent of the oxygen in water
also act as the primary food on the food-chain for the forage fish such
as minnows, shad, and small perch, which in turn are the primary food
of bass. Where you find high parts-per-million water, you will have a
heavy concentration of oxygen generating systems. Where these are
found in large numbers you will have large numbers of bait fish con-
gregated. And where these gather in numbers, the bass will also congre-
gate. *Consequently, you will greatly increase your chances of catching
large numbers of bass by fishing the areas of high PPM oxygen*—the
oxygen maximums.

Most likely, you and I have been spending two-thirds of our fishing
time fishing fishable but fishless water. That's right! Fifty to eighty and
sometimes ninety percent of the fishable water in today's natural lakes,
streams, impoundments, and rivers cannot possibly contain fish. Two
out of every three or four casts or two out of every three areas we fish
probably won't hold our prey, because there is not enough oxygen to
keep them alive.

Do not assume that all weed beds, moss fields, or duck weed covered
water will be an area of high oxygen. Many times these "fishy-looking"
areas will be oxygen-deficient if not entirely anoxic (without oxygen).
*Also, do not assume that an oxygen maximum area today will also be
one tomorrow.* This is not true. Many times—due to a host of environ-
mental conditions—oxygen maximum areas will change overnight. Similarly, many times a shoreline or offshore area that wasn't an oxygen
maximum one day will become one by the next time you go fishing.

After reading the *BASSmaster* article, which was prepared by a staff
writer after an intensive test program, I was reluctant to believe that I may
have been fishing bassless waters—even potential hot spots located with the
aid of depth finders and other gadgets! But it's true. I bought an oxygen
monitor and was surprised at the difference in PPM readings from one part
of the lake to the next. My conclusion is that bass fishing will shortly be

revolutionized. Again. And the bassman will have these new terms in his growing vocabulary:

Oxygen maximum. Although bass may exist in comfort at from 5 to 13 PPM, they will be more active in high PPM. An "oxygen maximum" is usually from 8 to 13 PPM, but the term is relative. If a given lake on a given day had no spot with more than 7.5 PPM, then that figure would be the oxygen maximum.

Oxycline. As shown in Figure 101, there may be a definite line, or interface, in some lakes that separates good oxygen water from bad. It's called the oxycline, and it can be independent of both temperature and bottom contour. In addition it may vary in depth from one part of the lake to another.

It is believed that microscopic life will gather closely along the oxycline and that forage fish will bunch up here. Of course, the bass will also move in to feed.

Intermediate maximum. Some lakes may not have a clearly defined oxycline on some days. If not, there *may* be an "intermediate maximum," as shown in Figure 102. It is simply a layer that has a higher PPM reading than the layer above and below it.

Oxygen inversion. As of this writing, I haven't located an "oxygen inversion," a highly oxygenated layer under an anoxic zone, as shown in Figure 103. According to the *BASSmaster* article:

> This third layer, caused by abrupt changes in barometric pressure, underwater currents, wind direction, wind velocity, and fluctuations of a host of other environmental conditions, lies just under the oxygen depleted zone and is fairly high in oxygen content, usually from 8 to 12 PPM. It is formed by the oxycline rolling under the previously existing layer of anoxic water.
>
> This oxygen inversion is usually found either near a sharp drop-off or in association with underground springs. When such an inversion is formed, the fish are trapped within this "pocket" of highly oxygenated water in a fairly confined area. These inversions form quickly and will last only for a few days. When you do find an inversion, hang on.

Note carefully that on certain days some lakes may not have an oxycline, an oxygen inversion, an intermediate maximum, and possibly not even an oxygen maximum. In this case, you would be likely to find bass scattered all over the lake, but of course the big ones will more than likely be in or near deep-water structure or under heavy cover near deep water.

When you do find an oxycline or an intermediate-maximum layer, your

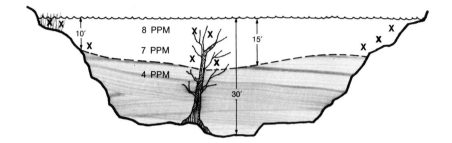

Figure 101

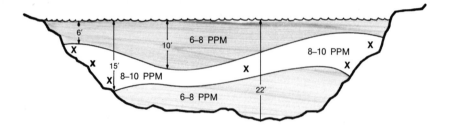

Figure 102

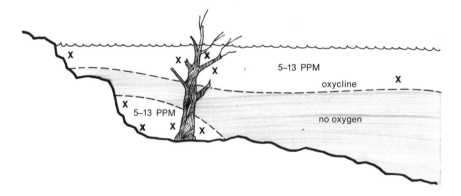

Figure 103

best fishing will be where the interface or the layer intersects with suitable structure. Such a situation is shown in Figure 104. And your fantastic fishing will occur when you put it all together by locating a spot where the oxygen content, structure, light intensity, and temperature are all optimum. On the other hand, you could go out for a day's fishing and end up not wetting a line because you spent all your time looking for the ideal spot!

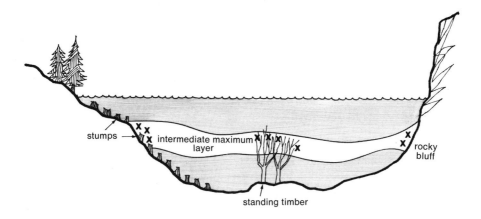

Figure 104

Although I'm convinced that the oxygen monitor is one of the more useful gadgets available to the modern bassman, I have to admit that I bought mine with some misgivings. Sometimes I feel that we're getting too many gadgets and we spend too much fishing time running around the lake making readings with depth finders, temperature gauges, light meters, and oxygen monitors. Sometimes I have an urge to leave all this stuff at home and just go fishing. Sometimes I do just that—and I catch bass that way (sometimes).

Another misgiving I have about the new oxygen monitor, and all the other electronic gadgets, is that a lot of serious fishermen simply can't afford them. To these anglers I want to point out that a lot of bass can be caught without all the gadgets, and I sometimes suspect that it may be more enjoyable. An angler without the gadgets is *fishing* for bass, whereas one with all the modern equipment is *hunting* for bass. Indeed, some of the new breed of bassmen enjoy the hunt more than the catch. It's a separate sport, really. In any case, the angler who doesn't have all the electronic gear should not feel that he can't locate bass. If he has rod, reel, line, and lure, then he has the greatest fish finder ever devised!

Appendixes

Guide to the Basses

THE LARGEMOUTH BASS *(Micropterus salmoides)*

Of the several black basses, the largemouth is the easiest to identify. Its lower jaw juts back past the eye, as shown in Figure 105. Also, there is a separation between the soft and spiny dorsal fins, as shown in Figure 106. Coloration varies considerably from largemouth to largemouth, locale to locale, but the largemouth is usually blackish or greenish. Most specimens have dark, splotched bands down either side from head to tail, but the band may be more or less obscured, especially on older fish.

The largemouth's original range was from Florida to Mexico, and up the Mississippi valley into Canada. Its range extended up the Atlantic Coast to Maryland. Until transplanted, it did not extend west of the Rockies or into the New England states. But it has been introduced, and is now thriving, in all states except Alaska. It has also been introduced in several foreign countries, including Japan and France.

Although the largemouth is a hearty fish, is quite adaptable, and spawns readily in various parts of the country, it shows a marked preference for waters having good cover and underwater structure, as has been stressed throughout this book. The largemouth does quite well in weedy lakes and

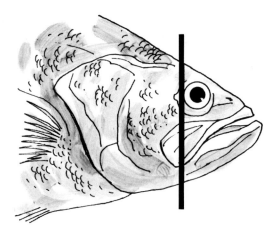

largemouth bass

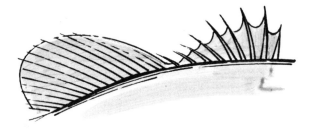

Figure 105

streams, whereas the smallmouth bass and the spotted bass prefer rocky lakes and streams.

The world's record largemouth bass is 22 pounds 4 ounces, caught in 1932 from Lake Montgomery, Georgia. The average size of adult specimens varies widely from North to South. They grow bigger in the South simply because the warmer water keeps their metabolic rate high throughout most of the year. In Florida, 10-pounders are common, but they would be real lunkers in northern states.

Actually, the Florida bass is almost certainly a separate fish, and it grows larger than other largemouths when it is in suitable waters. The range of the Florida bass, which extends up into South Georgia and South Alabama, has been extended, or jumped, to Southern California. Since being stocked in 1960, the Florida bass is doing extremely well in the city lake system

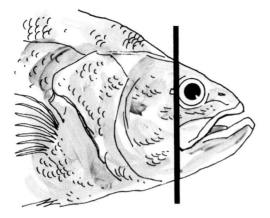

smallmouth bass

Figure 106

around San Diego. The transplanted bass have, in fact, been breaking California state records almost every year:

1968	14 pounds 15 ounces
1969	15 pounds 4 ounces
1971	16 pounds 11 ounces
1972	17 pounds 14 ounces
1973	20 pounds 15 ounces

Will the next world's record largemouth come from California? Some people think so, although there are probably several record breakers in the so-called big-bass belt, which extends from Central Florida northward into South Georgia and South Alabama.

THE SMALLMOUTH BASS *(Micropterus dolomieui)*

The smallmouth *does* have a slightly smaller mouth than the largemouth, but the difference is not large enough for positive identification. One obvious comparative feature is that the smallmouth's upper jaw does not extend back beyond the eye, as is shown in Figure 106. There is not as deep a notch between the soft and spiny dorsal fins. The adult smallmouth specimens usually have a bronze cast, and the length of their bodies is marked with dark, vertical bars.

According to *McClane's Standard Fishing Encyclopedia:*

The range of the smallmouth is from Minnesota to Quebec and south to northern Alabama, then west to eastern Kansas and Oklahoma. It has been introduced in many other states from coast to coast.

The geography of the smallmouth bass can be traced by the growth of American railroads. Until the year 1869, its range was largely confined to the Lake Ontario and Ohio River drainage systems, but as the wood-burning diamond stackers rolled south and west, the bass became a commuter. The original brood of the Potomac basin, for example, came from the Ohio River by riding over the Alleghenies on the Baltimore and Ohio in a bucket hanging in the water tender. This resulted in some widely scattered plantings, and eventually the smallmouth arrived in California from Lake Ontario via New York.

The smallmouth is usually found in rocky locations in lakes and streams. They prefer clear, rocky lakes with a minimum depth of 25–30 feet and with temperatures in the summer no less than 60 degrees F, and no more than 80 degrees F. In streams, this bass prefers a good percentage of riffles flowing over gravel, boulders, or bedrock.

Perhaps the most outstanding area from the standpoint of record or near-record fish is in southern TVA impoundments, such as Dale Hollow Reservoir bordering Kentucky and Tennessee, or Wheeler Dam in Alabama. These lakes produce smallmouths in the 8-pound class every season. By contrast, the dedicated light-tackle man seeks his fishing in rivers like the Delaware in New York and New Jersey, the North Branch of the Susquehanna in Pennsylvania, the Rappahannock and James in Virginia, Ohio's Whetstone, the Elkhorn, Kinninick, and Green of Kentucky, or the St. Croix in Wisconsin. There is little chance of hooking heavy smallmouths in these running waters. A 4-pounder would be exceptional. But the thrill of drifting a bug over strong and oftentimes selective fish epitomizes the fly-rod game. The smallmouth is a fish of large lakes, and it prefers water that is clear and rocky such as that found in southeastern Maine, which is noted for its May to June bass fishing. A good spot to locate bronzebacks is over gravel bars between submerged weed beds in 10–20-foot depths. You will also find bass at the dropoff near shale banks and on the gravel points which run out from shore. Another hot spot is the reefs which often occur far out in a large lake. You may find mounds of rock rising near the surface many miles from shore. Smallmouths regularly hunt crayfish on these shoals, particularly in the Great Lakes region.

The world's record smallmouth bass is 11 pounds 15 ounces, caught in 1955 from Dale Hollow Lake, Kentucky.

THE SPOTTED BASS *(Micropterus punctulatus)*

Also called Kentucky bass, the spotted bass has some characteristics similar to both the smallmouth and the largemouth. Its lower jaw does not extend beyond the eye, but it does extend farther than the smallmouth's; usually, the spotted bass's lower jaw juts back about midway between the two extremes shown in Figure 105. The spotted bass is usually identified by rows of small spots below the lateral line, formed by scales with dark bases.

The range of the spotted bass includes the Ohio and the Mississippi River systems all the way to the Gulf of Mexico. In the West, it is found as far as Texas, Oklahoma, and Kansas; in the East, as far as the Apalachicola River system in Florida. Some of the best states for the spotted bass include Alabama, Tennessee, Arkansas, and Kentucky. In some locations, the spotted bass is an important species for anglers; for example, 60 to 80 percent of the black bass caught from Georgia's Lake Allatoona are spotted bass. The spotted bass likes deep water, especially along steep banks and bluffs. It also shows a marked preference for rocks and rocky structure.

The world's record is 8 pounds 10½ ounces, taken in 1972 from Lake Lewis Smith in Alabama.

THE REDEYE BASS *(Micropterus coosae)*

The redeye bass and subspecies are also known as Flint River smallmouths, Chipola bass, shoal bass, and Coosa bass. Although the differences between subspecies are difficult to discern, the redeye bass generally looks like a smallmouth. It does have discernible color patterns, but the surest identifying feature of mature specimens is the red color of their eyes. Their soft dorsal, anal, and caudal fins are also reddish.

The redeye is a stream bass, and its range includes the drainage and upland tributaries of the following river systems: the Chattahoochee and Flint in Georgia; the Alabama–Coosa–Tallapoosa system in Alabama; the Savannah in Georgia; the Conasauga in Tennessee; and the Chipola in Florida. It prefers small, swift, rocky streams and will not spawn in lakes and ponds.

The weight of the redeye, complicated by somewhat disputed subspecies, varies considerably from one river to another. The world's record is 6 pounds ½ ounce, caught in 1967 on Hallawakee Creek in Lee County, Alabama.

THE SUWANNEE BASS *(Micropterus notius)*

This small bass seldom exceeds 10 or 12 inches in length. It has some markings similar to the redeye and the spotted bass, and other markings similar to the smallmouth. But the Suwannee bass can usually be identified by a blue color on its lower belly, and most specimens have dark, diamond-shaped blotches along the sides.

The Suwannee bass grows in the Suwannee River system of Florida, which includes the Sante Fe River, the Ichtucknee River, and the Withlacoochee River in Madison County (not to be confused with the larger Withlacoochee River in Central Florida). The Suwannee bass has also been identified in the Ochlockonee River. Probably the best place to catch the Suwannee bass is in the Sante Fe River, where it represents about 30 percent of the black bass taken by anglers.

No official world's record is maintained, but the largest one known (according to *Florida Wildlife,* February 1973) had a length of 13.5 inches and weighed 1.7 pounds. Although the Suwannee bass is small, it has a reputation as a real fighter, and it makes good sport on fly-rod or ultralight spinning gear.

Directory
of Tackle
Manufacturers

Code: 1, rods and reels; 2, fishing lines; 3, lures; 4, fishing accessories; 5, electronic aids

Tony Accetta & Son, 3
932 Avenue E
Riviera Beach, Fla. 33404

Aitken-Warner Corporation, 3, 4
427 Beech Street
Green Camp, Ohio 43322

Al's Goldfish Lure Company, 3, 4
516 Main Street
Indian Orchard, Mass. 01051

Fred Arbogast Company, Inc., 3, 4
313 W. North Street
Akron, Ohio 44303

The Arnold Tackle Corp., 3, 4
Paw Paw, Mich. 49079

B & B Tackle Company, 3, 4
1600 W. Frank Street
Lufkin, Texas 75901

Jim Bagley Bait Company, 3
P. O. Box 110
Winter Haven, Fla. 33880

Bass Buster, Inc., 3
301 Main Street
Amsterdam, Mo. 64723

Berkley & Co., Inc., 1, 2
Highways 9 and 71
Spirit Lake, Iowa 51360

Best Tackle Mfg. Co., 2, 3, 4
3106 Bay Street
Unionville, Mich. 48767

Betts Tackle, Ltd., 3
Highway 42 West
Fuquay-Varina, N.C. 27526

Blakemore, 3
P.O. Box 505
Branson, Mo. 65616

Bomber Bait Company, 3
Gainesville, Texas 76240

Boone Bait Company, Inc., 3
P.O. Box 571
Winter Park, Fla. 32789

Browning Mfg. Co., 1
Route 1
Morgan, Utah 84050

Brunswick Corp., 1, 3, 4
1 Brunswick Plaza
Skokie, Ill. 60602

Buck's Baits, 3
P.O. Box 66
Hickory, N.C. 28601

Burke Flexo-Products, 3, 4
1969 S. Airport Road
Traverse City, Mich, 49684

Byrd Industries Inc., 5
201 Rock Industrial Park Drive
Bridgeton, Mo. 63044

Lew Childre & Sanders, Inc.,
  1, 4
P.O. Box 535
Foley, Ala. 36535

Cisco Kid Tackle, Inc., 3
2630 N.W. 1st Avenue
Boca Raton, Fla 33432

Cordell Tackle, Inc., 3, 4
P.O. Box 2020
Hot Springs, Ark. 71901

Cortland Line Co., 1, 2, 4
67 E. Court Street
Cortland, N.Y. 13045

Creek Chub Bait Co., 3
E. Keyser Street
Garrett, Ind. 46738

Creme Lure Company, 3
P.O. Box 87
Tyler, Texas 75701

Daisy, 1, 3, 4
P.O. Box 220
Rogers, Ark. 72756

Daiwa Corporation, 1, 2
14011 S. Normandie
Gardena, Calif. 90247

Les Davis Fishing Tackle Co.,
  2, 3, 4
1565 Center Street
Tacoma, Wash. 98409

DeLong Lures, Inc., 3
80 Compark Road
Centerville, Ohio 45459

E. I. Du Pont de Nemours &
   Co., Inc., 2
1007 Market Street
Wilmington, Del. 19810

Eagle Claw
See Wright & McGill Company

Lou J. Eppinger Mfg. Co., 3
6340 Schaefer Highway
Dearborn, Mich. 48126

Fenwick
See Sevenstrand Tackle Mfg. Co.

Fishmaster Products, Inc., 5
P.O. Box 9635
Tulsa, Okla. 74107

Fo-Mac, Inc., 4, 5
2621 N. Iroquois Street
Tulsa, Okla. 47106

Four Rivers Tackle Co., 3, 4
410 Eleventh Street
Greenwood, Miss. 38930

G & R Industries, Inc., 3, 5
P.O. Box 18
Purdy, Mo. 65734

The Gaines Company, 3
P.O. Box 35
Gaines, Pa. 16921

Gapen Tackle Company, 3, 4
Highway 10
Big Lake, Minn. 55309

The Garcia Corporation, 1, 2, 3, 5
329 Alfred Avenue
Teaneck, N.J. 07666

Gladding Corporation, 1, 2, 3, 4, 5
P.O. Box 586
Boston, Mass. 02117

Gudebrod Bros. Silk Co., Inc., 2, 3, 4
12 S. 12th Street
Philadelphia, Pa. 19107

Harrison-Hoge Industries, Inc.,
   1, 2, 3, 4
104 Arlington Avenue
St. James, N.Y. 11780

Heddon, 1, 3, 4
414 West Street
Dowagiac, Mich. 49047

Helin Tackle Company, 3
4099 Beaufait
Detroit, Mich. 48207

John J. Hildebrandt Corp., 3
P.O. Box 50
Logansport, Ind. 46947

The Hofschneider Corp., 3
848 Jay Street
Rochester, N.Y. 14611

Hopkins Lure Company, 3
1130 Boissevain Avenue
Norfolk, Va. 23507

Ray Jefferson, 5
Main and Cotton Streets
Philadelphia, Pa. 19127

Luhr Jensen & Sons, Inc., 3, 4
P.O. Box 297
Hood River, Ore. 97031

Padre Island Co., 3
2617 N. Zarzamora Street
San Antonio, Texas 78201

E. H. Peckinpaugh Co., 3
P.O. Box 15044
Baton Rouge, La. 70815

Pedigo Pork Rind Co., Inc., 3, 4
500 W. 10th Street
Bowling Green, Ky. 42101

Penn Fishing Tackle Mfg. Co., 1
3028 W. Hunting Park Avenue
Philadelphia, Pa. 19132

Pflueger Sporting Goods, 1, 2,
   3, 4, 5
P.O. Box 310
Hallandale, Fla. 33009

Phillips Fly & Tackle Co., 3
P.O. Box 188
Alexandria, Pa. 16611

Plano Molding Company, 4
P.O. Box 189
Plano, Ill. 60545

Eddie Pope & Co., Inc., 3, 4
25572 Stanford Avenue
Valencia, Calif. 91355

Pro Bass Anglers Tackle Company,
   3, 4
10089 Washington Church Road
Miamisburg, Ohio 45342

Quick Corp. of America, 1
620 Terminal Way
Costa Mesa, Calif. 92627

Ranger Tackle Co., Inc., 3
P.O. Box 6383 South Station
Fort Smith, Ark. 72901

Rebel Lures, 3
Box 1587
Fort Smith, Ark. 72901

Recreational Development, Inc., 1, 3
201 Mill Branch Road
Tallahassee, Fla. 32303

Rogers, 3
P.O. Box 142
Lamar, Mo. 64759

Scientific Anglers, Inc., 1, 2, 4
4100 James Savage Road
Midland, Mich. 48640

Sevenstrand Tackle Mfg. Co., 1, 2, 3, 4
14799 Chestnut Street
Westminster, Calif. 92683

Shakespeare Company, 1, 2, 3, 4, 5
241 E. Kalamazoo Avenue
Kalamazoo, Mich. 49001

Shannon Lure Co., 3
3654 W. Montrose Avenue
Chicago, Ill. 60618

Sheldon's, Inc.
P.O. Box 508
Antigo, Wis. 54409

Jack K. Smithwick & Son, 3
P.O. Box 1205
Shreveport, La. 71163

South Bend
See Gladding Corporation

Sportsman's Products, Inc., 3
841 E. 38th Street
Marion, Ind. 46952

Steffey Mfg. Co.
404 Martin Drive
Irwin, Pa. 15642

Stembridge Products, Inc.
2941 Central Avenue
East Point, Ga. 30344

Storm Mfg. Co., 3
P.O. Box 265
Norman, Okla. 73069

T & D Tackle Co., 3
P.O. Box 1252
Melbourne, Fla. 32901

Tiki Lures, Inc., 3
1805 E. Eleven Mile Road
Madison Heights, Mich. 48071

True Temper Corp., 1
1623 Euclid Avenue
Cleveland, Ohio 44115

UMCO Corporation, 4
Highway 25, Box 608
Watertown, Minn. 55388

Uncle Josh Bait Company, 3
524 Clarence Street
Fort Atkinson, Wis. 53538

Vexilar, Inc., 5
9345 Penn Ave., S.
Minneapolis, Minn. 55431

Vlchek Plastics Co., 4
P.O. Box 97
Middlefield, Ohio 44062

Waller Corp., 5
4220 Stickney Street
Crystal Lake, Ill. 60014

Weber Tackle Co., 3, 4
Stevens Point, Wis. 54481

Weed Master, 4
P.O. Box 5252
Fort Lauderdale, Fla. 33310

Erwin Weller Co., 3, 4
2105 Clark Street
Sioux City, Iowa 51104

Whopper Stopper, Inc., 3
P.O. Box 1111
Sherman, Texas 75090

Woodstream Corp., 1, 2, 3, 4
P.O. Box 327
Lititz, Pa. 17543

The Worth Company, 3, 4
P.O. Box 88
Stevens Point, Wis. 54481

Wright & McGill Company, 1, 2
4245 E. 46th Avenue
Denver, Colo. 80216

Yakima Bait Co., 2, 3
P.O. Box 310
Granger, Wash. 98932

Zebco, 1, 2, 3
6101 E. Apache Street
Tulsa, Okla. 74115

Zorro Bait Co., 3
1315 51st Avenue N
Nashville, Tenn. 37209

Directory
of Bass Boat
Manufacturers

Allison Craft Boats
Route 1
Box 1
Louisville, Tenn. 37777

Arrowglass Boats
931 Firestone Building
Memphis, Tenn. 38107

Astroglass Boat Company
Box 7
Pleasant View, Tenn. 37146

Bassmaster Boats
Box 175
Junction City, Ky. 40440

Boston Whaler, Inc.
1149 Hingham Street
Rockland, Mass. 02370

Chrysler Marine
Box 1919
Detroit, Mich. 48231

Crestliner Boats
609 13th Avenue, N.E.
Little Falls, Minn. 56345

Crosby Aeromarine Co.
5203 W. Highway 98
Panama City, Fla. 32401

Delhi Mfg. Corp.
Delhi, La. 71232

Ebbtide Boat Company
White Bluff, Tenn. 37187

Fabuglas Co., Inc.
6401 Centennial Boulevard
Nashville Tenn. 37209

Fisher Marine, Inc.
P.O. Box 1256
West Point, Miss. 39773

Forrest Wood Mfg. Co.
Flippin, Ark. 72634

Glastron Boat Company
P.O. Box 9447
Austin, Texas 78766

Gold Line
1507 Independence Street
Cape Girardeau, Mo. 63701

Hosea Mfg. Co.
Quitman, Texas 75783

Hydra-Sports
13th and G Streets
Smyrna, Tenn. 37167

MFG
Union City, Pa. 16438

Master Molders, Inc.
P.O. Box 815
Clarksville, Texas 75426

MonArk Boat Company
P.O. Box 210
Monticello, Ark. 71655

Ouachita Marine and Industrial
721 Main Street
Little Rock, Ark. 72201

Polar Kraft Mfg. Co.
P.O. Box 708
Olive Branch, Miss. 38654

Ray-Craft
P.O. Box 596
San Augustine, Texas 75972

Rebel Boats
3610 Jenny Lind Road
Fort Smith, Ark. 72901

Skeeter
P.O. Box 1205
Longview, Texas 75601

Starcraft Company
2703 College Avenue
Goshen, Ind. 16526

Tide Craft
P.O. Box 796
Minden, La. 71055

Warrior Fiberglass Products
Box 929
Jasper, Ala. 35501

Index